trotman

Teaching

UNCOVERED

Teaching Uncovered

This first edition published in 2006 by Trotman and Company Ltd
2 The Green, Richmond, Surrey TW9 1PL

© Trotman and Company Limited 2006

Editorial and Publishing Team

Authors Brin Best and Siân Dover
Editorial Mina Patria, Editorial Director; Jo Jacomb, Editorial
Manager; Catherine Travers, Managing Editor; Ian Turner,
Editorial Assistant
Production Ken Ruskin, Head of Manufacturing and Logistics;
James Rudge, Production Artworker
Advertising Tom Lee, Commercial Director

Designed by XAB

British Library Cataloguing in Publication Data
A catalogue record for this book is available from the British Library

ISBN 1 84455 090 7

Typeset by Mac Style, Nafferton, East Yorkshire
Printed and bound by Creative Design and Print Group, Wales

CONTENTS

About the Authors

BRIN BEST

Brin worked as a secondary school teacher and head of department for eight years before joining the advisory team of a local education authority. Since 2002 he has been the director of Innovation for Education Ltd, an education training and consultancy company based in Yorkshire. He speaks and writes widely on a variety of education issues, and is the author or editor of a range of other books on education issues. He is the series consultant for the *Teachers' Pocketbooks*, which won a British Educational Resource Award in 2005. He is a member of the Chartered Institute of Journalists and a Fellow of the Royal Geographical Society. Brin is studying part-time for a doctorate in education, investigating effective teaching and learning methods.

SIÂN DOVER

Siân is in her tenth year as a secondary school teacher and has been the joint head of a PE department for the past two years. She is also a mentor for students on the Graduate Training Programme and for Newly Qualified Teachers at her school. Siân has a degree in Physical Education and Geography and a secondary PGCE in Physical Education. She is currently doing a conversion course, studying for the Certificate in Primary Education. She went part-time after having her two children and now teaches three days a week, as well as carrying out educational consultancy and writing. She contributed a chapter to the highly acclaimed *Gifted and Talented Co-ordinator's Handbook*. Later this year she will take up a post as a school sports co-ordinator, a role that aims to promote and encourage participation in physical education.

Acknowledgements

We are very grateful to those people who took the time to be interviewed for the book. Their real life profiles help to convey the excitement and challenges of teaching. Gill O'Donnell compiled the quotes and facts dotted throughout the book, and helped in innumerable other ways to improve the content of the book. She has been a constant source of support in the Innovation for Education office throughout the project.

From Andrew Flintoff to Meera Syal, Charlotte Church to Benjamin Zephaniah, James Dyson to Ellen MacArthur, leading figures in our country have paid tribute to the vital role of their teachers in shaping their careers.

'I suppose Jane Latozel was like all the best teachers in that what she gave you went beyond just teaching, or beyond the classroom. It was a view of the world, and a view of yourself in the world.'

Kwame Kwei-Armah, actor, singer and playwright

Teaching has rightly been described as one of this country's most important professions – but what is it **really** like to be a teacher? How do you get into teaching? What are the rewards and challenges? In *Teaching Uncovered* you'll find the answers to these and many other questions that will help you decide whether a career in teaching is really for you.

FASCINATING FACTS

At the start of the third millennium there were 34,368 schools in the UK.

In *Teaching Uncovered* you'll find:

- information about the various roles within teaching

- guidance on the skills, qualifications and training you'll need as a teacher

- interviews with, and profiles of, real teachers

- advice on what to do next if you're ready to take on the challenge of teaching.

THE SCOPE OF THIS BOOK

This book focuses on the career of teaching from nursery to secondary level. It also outlines the range of support roles that teachers can go on to do. Although it is not specifically targeted at teaching in further education colleges or in education settings outside schools, there is much in *Teaching Uncovered* that is also relevant to these wider teaching roles. The main emphasis of the book is on teaching in UK schools that are funded by the government (called state or maintained schools), rather than in independent schools where fees have to be paid by parents.

'It's always rewarding to see those students who have excelled at school do well, but I find it even more impressive when young people who've struggled manage to achieve their goals – this is when teaching really is the best job in the world!'

Kitty Pollit, teacher, Manchester

MAKING YOUR DECISION

The main aim of *Teaching Uncovered* is to help you make an informed decision about whether teaching is the right career choice for you. By explaining the range of roles that are now possible, we want to encourage you to think carefully about which route seems most appropriate for you, taking account of your background, interests and skills.

'I saw Mrs Peters as a special auntie, someone I could talk to and completely trusted. I tell my children about her because I think it's important that they find a special teacher. That kind of relationship can have an enormous effect on the rest of their lives.'

Karren Brady, Managing Director of Birmingham City FC

ANSWERS AND QUESTIONS

We hope to provide answers to some of the burning questions you have about teaching. But we also want to get you to ask yourself some key questions, such as:

- Am I really cut out to be a teacher?

- What skills and qualities do I have that are relevant?

- Could I handle the pressure?

- Is this the right step for me just now?

Only you can answer these questions, and your answers should ultimately determine whether you decide to start out on a career in teaching. While we can't provide you with the answers to these critical questions, we can support you with information, advice and thought-provoking tools that will enable you to make up your mind. Careful reflection is an important feature of the book.

In April 2003 the smallest school in the UK was registered on Papa Stour in the Shetland Islands. It consisted of one teacher and one student.

Remember that there's no substitute for actually experiencing teaching in all its forms, so in addition to reading this book, we strongly recommend you gain some practical experience. This could involve observing lessons at a school where you already have links. It might also encompass shadowing someone in a post that interests you, or even carrying out a proper work experience placement for a more lengthy period.

THE HIGHS AND LOWS OF TEACHING

'Teaching can be the best and the worst job in the world, all in the space of a week. It really is a rollercoaster for the emotions. This was illustrated during one exhausting week in May whilst I was a teacher at a comprehensive school. A student in my form with special educational needs (Jack) had reached a huge milestone by never having had a day off school since he was four. Everyone at the school was amazed by Jack's achievement and keen to celebrate what he had done, so we telephoned the local newspaper to set up a photo. We hadn't realised just how unusual Jack's achievement was, as within a few hours we had all the major newspapers telephoning us and even Sky TV wanting to film him!

'The next morning Jack had his own page in all the tabloid newspapers and was interviewed for several radio stations. He even had his own page on Ceefax! It was a huge vote of confidence for Jack, who had tried so hard during his time as a student and was very popular with staff and other students. Jack's parents, who had supported him so well throughout, were of course very proud of their son, and pleased that his achievements had been recognised so widely. They accompanied him to Leeds to film for the early evening Calendar programme.

'The euphoria of Jack's achievements seemed a distant memory on the Friday, however, when the whole school was shocked to hear that a student had taken an overdose because she had been repeatedly bullied. There were serious accusations from her parents that the school had not done enough to address the problem, and every member of staff began to question if there was anything else they should have done to help. Not many of us slept that well over the weekend, hoping the student would recover.

'Thankfully, the student did eventually recover from her overdose, but the incident cast a dark shadow over the rest of the term, and helped to take the edge off the high of Jack's achievement. Though I still continued to love teaching, the week helped to illustrate why it is such an exciting but draining profession. Prepare yourself for your own emotional rollercoaster!'

Lucy Butters, Norfolk

FASCINATING FACTS

In 2005 16% of all calls to the Teacher Support Network were in relation to workplace stress. The commonest causes of stress were relationships with colleagues and managers, excessive workload and student indiscipline.

TO GET YOU THINKING

Before launching into the book proper, we invite you to pause here to consider what you already know about teaching. This will help you get more out of the book by merging what you're about to learn with your existing knowledge, so have a go at the following:

● Make a list of as many types of teacher as you can think of. (You could try to categorise these by age, subject, place of work etc.)

● What do you think are the chief qualities of a really good teacher? Your own experiences as a student will help here

● What attracts you to teaching as a career, based on what you already know about it? Are there any challenges you know teachers face that concern you? Why?

● Jot down some key questions about teaching that you need to know the answers to. You'll need to look out for the answers to these as you read through the book

● Think about the key things you want to gain by reading this book, and write them down. These are your 'learning goals'.

CHAPTER 1

The background to schools and teaching

Teachers have a major influence on our lives. Far more than simply being the people who help us to pass exams, teachers can inspire us, help to shape our values, challenge our thinking and frequently provide us with role models to raise our aspirations.

In the hectic modern life of the twenty-first century, teachers often spend more face-to-face time with young people than their parents do. And nobody can deny the huge boost to a young person's life that a truly dedicated teacher can provide.

'Mrs Cogbill had this attitude simply to get out there and do it. At the time there wasn't much talk about "inclusion", but she didn't treat me any differently from anyone else and just encouraged me to get on with it. I joined my local athletics club when I was 15 and trained at school. Even back then the idea of me being a disabled athlete didn't seem strange to them. When I look back now I think it was way ahead of its time. It was that sort of school.'
Tanni Grey-Thompson, multi-gold medal-winning athlete

TEACHERS AND PLACES OF LEARNING

In the UK, in common with other economically developed nations, formal compulsory education for children and young people takes place in four phases (see table). The vast majority of teachers tend to specialise in one particular phase, and the training required to work in that phase is quite specific.

FASCINATING FACTS

When La Crosse School District in western Kansas tried to give away its former middle school to more than 40 charities, there were no takers – so they sold it on eBay instead for $49,500!

PHASE	SCHOOL TYPE	MILESTONES
Pre-primary	Nursery schools; some primary schools have nurseries attached	Children are referred to as being in the 'Foundation Stage' at ages 3–5 before entering key stage 1 at primary school
Primary *The age of transition to a primary school is usually 5*	Primary schools*	**Key stage 1 SATs** at age 7 (reading; writing (handwriting/spelling); maths); **key stage 2 SATs** at age 11 (reading; writing/handwriting; spelling; maths; mental arithmetic; science)
Secondary *The age of transition to a secondary school is usually 11*	Secondary schools*	**Key stage 3 SATs** at age 14 (English (reading, writing, one Shakespeare play); maths; science), **GCSEs** at age 16, **vocational qualifications**
Tertiary *The age of transition to a sixth-form or college of further education is usually 16*	Secondary schools with integral sixth-form colleges; colleges of further education; universities	A levels/International Baccalaureate at age 17–18; **advanced vocational qualifications**; some colleges also offer study to a more advanced level (e.g. degrees); **degrees** and other qualifications above A level

Notes: The key stages of education correspond to ages as follows: key stage 1, age 5–7; key stage 2, age 7–11; key stage 3, age 11–14; key stage 4, age 14–16. SATs are compulsory examinations taken at age 7, 11 and 14.
*Middle schools sometimes cover the age range from 9 to 13 or 14.

For those students who choose to continue their education beyond the age of 18, university (or a college of further education that offers a degree) is usually the next step. Here they will mix with older, 'mature' students (over 21 years old) who are returning to study after some years in the world of work.

FELICITY HAYNES, TEACHING ASSISTANT (PRIMARY)
This interview explains the vital role that teaching assistants carry out in schools, supporting the work of teachers. Some teaching assistants choose to progress into more senior roles, and in Felicity's case into teaching itself, via a variety of routes.

What is your current role in education?
'I'm currently working as a teaching assistant, which involves supporting the teacher in the classroom.'

When did you first become interested in working in education?
'I first thought I might pursue a career in teaching when I was in the sixth form at school. I had done some work experience in a school and thoroughly enjoyed it.'

Why did you decide to work in this particular area?
'After I'd completed my geography degree, rather than go straight into a PGCE I wanted to spend some more time working in schools so I could get a better idea of what being a teacher really involves.'

What qualifications/training do you have relevant to the role?
'I have a degree in geography. I've also done other training whilst I have been working, which includes courses on First Aid for People Working with Children, TOPS outdoors (PE training), and Speech Therapy and Language Communication.'

What particular skills are required for the job?
'There are a number of skills required for the job. These include tolerance, confidence, common sense and a good general knowledge. The job also involves teamwork but you must also be able to work independently using your own initiative.'

Describe a typical day
'I start work at 9am. The first half of the morning until break (this is at 10.30am) I spend with class 3 (years 4 and 5). Sometimes I work in the classroom providing general support for the children or I may take a group of children for a spelling test or some extra help. My colleague and I then do break duty, which lasts for 15 minutes. For the second half of the morning, I am with class 1 (reception and year 1), again providing general support. Lunchtime is from 12 to 1pm. This should be a chance to sit down and talk to other colleagues but this rarely happens, as there are always interruptions, be it children or jobs that I need to catch up on! Straight after lunch is PE for class 3. PE is one of my strengths and I usually take a group to work with during this lesson. I then do afternoon break duty from 2.15 to 2.30pm. My working day finishes at 3pm. The last half hour I usually spend putting away the PE equipment and filling in accident forms!'

What are working conditions like?
'The days are relatively short as I finish at 3pm, but they are busy days and there is not often a chance to sit down and relax. The school holidays are a definite bonus. For the amount of responsibility required, the pay is extremely basic.'

What are the highs and lows?
'As with all jobs there are both high and low points. Seeing the children progress has to be one of the most rewarding points of the job. There is certainly never a dull moment in this career and the wide variety of activities that take place ensure that no two days are ever the same. On a low point the amount of paperwork is increasing and much time is taken up filling forms, which is not enjoyable. The pay is also poor for what you are expected to do.'

What advice would you give somebody interested in pursuing a career in this field?
'Gain as much work experience as possible in a variety of settings. Understand that the days are intense but compensated for by regular holidays.'

What could a job like this lead on to?
'The opportunities in education are wide. There are various levels of teaching assistant, starting from general, advanced, then on to a Higher Level Teaching Assistant.

'Providing you have a degree there is also the option to do a Postgraduate Certificate in Education. However, teaching prepares you for many other possible careers.'

TYPES OF SCHOOL

As well as different schools for children of different ages, within the UK there's a wide range of different types of school, depending on how children are selected for entry, how the school is funded and what subjects it specialises in teaching.

FASCINATING FACTS

Lakeside School in Seattle received a generous donation from a former 'old boy' in 2005 when Bill Gates, founder of Microsoft, gave them $40m (£22.5m). He left the school in 1973.

THE STATE SECTOR

Most children in the UK are educated at schools in the state or 'maintained' sector, which means the schools are funded mainly by the government. There are several different types of state school.

COMPREHENSIVE
A secondary school that admits students of all abilities, and therefore without any academic selection procedure. In England 86.8% of all students attend a comprehensive school.

GRAMMAR
A secondary school catering for children of higher academic ability, usually measured by the Eleven Plus examination.

FOUNDATION

In foundation schools the land and buildings are owned by a governing body, who are also responsible for running the school, and the local education authority funds the curriculum at the school. The governing body employs the staff and buys in and administers most of the support services. The students have to follow the national curriculum and the admissions policy is determined and administered by the governing body, in consultation with the local education authority.

FASCINATING FACTS

In 2004 parents groups raised £73 million for schools across the country through fund-raising efforts.

VOLUNTARY-AIDED

In a voluntary-aided school the land and buildings are normally owned by a voluntary organisation (usually a church), but the governing body is responsible for running the school. The school is funded partly by the local education authority, partly by the governing body and partly by the voluntary organisation. The staff are employed by the governing body and the local education authority provides the support services. The students follow the national curriculum and the admissions policy is determined by the governors in consultation with the local education authority.

FASCINATING FACTS

Nidderdale High School in Pateley Bridge, North Yorkshire has a rather unusual addition to its school site – it has its own windmill, which helps reduce electricity bills.

VOLUNTARY-CONTROLLED

In a voluntary-controlled school the land and buildings are owned by a voluntary organisation, usually a church, but the governing body is responsible for running the school. However, the school is funded by the local education authority, which also employs the staff and provides the support services. Students follow the national curriculum but admissions policy is usually determined and administered by the local education authority.

CITY TECHNOLOGY COLLEGES

City Technology Colleges (CTCs) are independent non-fee-paying schools and are situated in urban areas. There are only a limited number of CTCs in the country. The college is run in accordance with an agreement between the company that owns it and the Department for Education and Skills (DfES) and funded by the DfES and commercial sponsors. The governing body employs the staff and buys in and administers the support services. The students follow a curriculum that is similar to the national curriculum, with particular emphasis on technological and practical skills, and the admissions policy is determined and administered by the governing body.

SPECIALIST

Specialist schools have a particular focus on those subjects relating to their chosen specialism, but they must also meet the requirements of the national curriculum and deliver a broad and balanced education to all students. A mainstream school can apply to develop one of ten specialisms: arts; business and enterprise; engineering; humanities; languages; mathematics and computing; music; science; sports; technology. Schools can also combine any two specialisms.

CITY ACADEMIES

City academies are independently managed, all-ability schools. They are set up in disadvantaged areas by sponsors from business, charities or voluntary groups, in partnership with the DfES and local education authorities. In a city academy the DfES funds the school's running costs and the governing body employs the staff. The students do not have to follow the national curriculum.

FAITH

Faith schools are run in the same way as other mainstream state schools, but many incorporate more religious and spiritual elements into the curriculum than non-faith schools. There are currently around 7,000 faith schools in England, 600 secondary and 6,400 primary. The vast majority (6,955) are Christian, with 36 Jewish, five Muslim and two Sikh schools.

SPECIAL SCHOOLS

Special schools are provided for children with specific physical or mental problems or disabilities. However, in recent years there have been moves towards fully integrating many of these students in mainstream schooling.

'Miss Cope made me forget I was blind. She'd say: "Have a go, just try." At parents' evenings, she told my mother and father I could do anything I wanted.'
Denise Leigh, joint winner (with Jane Gilchrist) of Channel 4's *Operatunity*

BERYL DOYLE, TEACHER OF DEAF CHILDREN
What is your role in education?
'I'm a teacher of English in a special school for deaf children'

When did you first become interested in teaching?
'At school. I always wanted to be a teacher and was always "playing schools" when I was little.'

What is a typical day like?
'I usually arrive in school at about 8.30am. I double check all my lessons for the day, open any mail and do any photocopying that's needed. If I'm on duty then I go down to collect the students from where the taxis or buses drop them off. I register the students and collect in any dinner money for the week. Before break I teach two lessons, either as two singles or a double. At break if I'm on duty I go down to the cloakroom and ask another teacher to get me a coffee. I then have another two lessons before lunch which could be with children from ages eight to 16. Because of their additional difficulties there is often a support worker in the classroom. At the start of lunch I take the students down to the canteen where they are met by the dinner supervisors. I have an hour for lunch, which is usually taken up by liaison meetings with other staff or agencies or sometimes extra lessons for students. I would also try to find some time to reflect and evaluate the lessons from the morning for future reference.

There are another two lessons to teach after lunch and school finishes at 3.20pm. Twice a week there are meetings from 3.30 to 4.30pm and once they have finished I go back to my classroom and sort out anything from that day. I usually leave for home between 5 and 5.30pm. Once home I tend to have a drink, make the tea, and watch television for a while. I would then work for another two to four hours before going to bed.'

What hours do you work in an average week?
'This is very difficult to say. It's about 48 hours including meetings but if often depends on how much work I have to do at home that week.'

What qualifications/training do you have?
'I did the Certificate of Education in 1969, which was a three-year training course incorporating a main and subsidiary subject. It also included training for ten curriculum subjects. I later went on to do a BATOD which is the diploma for teachers of the deaf. This was two years in-service training. I also have the CACDP sign language certificate.'

What advice would you give to people interested in pursuing a career in this field?
'Go into a mainstream school first to get experience and keep up with what's going on in mainstream education. Go on as many courses as you can to broaden your outlook and knowledge. Read up a lot about the disability and gain a sound knowledge of it and its implications for learning.'

What are the highs and lows of the job?
'The highs are the achievements of small steps: when "the penny drops" it gives you a buzz when you know you have helped and enabled students to learn. The lows are the paperwork and the constant new initiatives, which make you think, "when will I have time to do all this and teach?"'

What could a job like yours lead to?
'Head of department, deputy head, headteacher, other areas of special needs, educational psychologist, or a consultant in special education. Signing skills could be used in colleges or as an interpreter.'

THE INDEPENDENT SECTOR

Parents who choose to opt out of the state system send their children to independent schools, which are run privately, without direct assistance from the government. Parents usually have to pay school fees, though bursaries are often available to help those with special talents. By the late 1990s, just over 7% of children in the UK attended private fee-paying schools. There are some 2,420 independent schools in the UK, with about 600,000 students.

The terminology relating to independent schools can be confusing. A group of long-established and prestigious independent schools are known as 'public schools'. In England and Wales these are generally fee-paying independent schools, but in Scotland a 'public' school is a state-maintained school, and independent schools are generally known as 'private' schools. Originally, English public schools stressed a classical education, character training and sports, but the curriculum is now more closely allied to state education, although they usually offer a wider range of subjects and have a lower student-to-teacher ratio. Independent schools do not have to follow the national curriculum. Most independent schools offer education to students who also live at the school in term time (boarders), as well as day students. Many independent schools are attended by children whose parents live abroad.

FASCINATING FACTS

The oldest public school in England is reputed to be the King's School, Canterbury, which was founded in the year 597.

Independent schools are not required to employ the key stage assessment tests, though many prep (junior) schools do use key stage 1 and 2 tests simply as a benchmark exercise. Students are, in most cases, prepared for the same final examinations (GCSE, A level and International Baccalaureate) as at state schools.

William Shakespeare never spoke English at school – all students had to speak in Latin and any boy using English was punished! Despite which, he may then have gone on to act as a private teacher/tutor for a short while before moving to London to act and write.

MOLLY SAWLEY, PRIMARY SCHOOL TEACHER (INDEPENDENT SCHOOL)

What is your role in education?
'Teacher of PE and geography in an Independent school.'

What is a typical day like?
'I get to work for about 8.15am and do a morning duty which involves looking after the children who come into school early. Lessons start at 9am. I teach all ages from 5 to 11 so who I teach and the activity I teach will vary. Class sizes are small, between seven and 12, and sometimes, for PE, we teach children from different year groups together. We also do quite a bit of team teaching where there are two of us on at the same time. This can be useful as it means we can sometimes split the group to take smaller classes or one of us can have a lesson to plan or mark, and swap the next week. School finishes at 4.15pm and I do a duty twice a week until 5.15pm where I supervise the children who stay for clubs.'

When did you first become interested in teaching?
'I thought that I would become a teacher from a young age but decided to keep my options open when I went to university so did a normal degree and then did teacher training after that.'

What hours do you work in an average week?
'I only work part time so about 20 hours a week.'

What qualifications do you have?
'A BA (Hons) in sport science and geography, and a PGCE in secondary PE.'

What advice would you give to somebody interested in pursuing a career in this field?
'Many teachers think that teaching in an independent school is easier or not as challenging. I don't think that is true. There are different challenges such as the parents who tend to get more involved as they are paying for their children's education. If I were honest I would probably say get some experience in a state school first and then go to an independent school if you want to. I think the feeling that if you have taught in an independent school then you can not go into the state sector has changed now. All teaching is difficult – make sure you really want to do it.'

What are the highs and lows of the job?
'The highs are the children you work with and the buzz you get when they achieve something. Also the holidays are good and the pay is reasonable now. The lows are the constant justification to parents about what you are doing and how their child is learning.'

What could a job like yours lead on to?
'You could work your way up to a deputy headteacher or a headteacher. You may just want to stay as a classroom teacher and move to a different school.'

LINKS BETWEEN SCHOOLS

Teachers in primary and secondary schools tend not to come into contact that much, unless their schools are involved in a joint project of some kind. The one area where there is consistent collaboration concerns transition – when primary school children move up to secondary school. Liaison meetings to make arrangements for transition help what is often a traumatic process for children run more smoothly.

The links between the state and independent sector are less strong still, though a recent government initiative to get them working more closely together – the Independent–State School Partnership – is helping to bridge the gap.

FASCINATING FACTS

Teaching is becoming a female profession. Statistics from the Secondary Headteachers Association show that there are 101,000 women secondary teachers to 88,000 men. However, men still dominate headships in secondary education, holding 70% of the total.

HOW SCHOOLS WORK

If you've spent any time as a student at a school in the UK in the last ten years or so, then you'll have a good idea of how things work from day to day. The staffing diagram shows who does what in a school. The diagram is typical of the state sector: in independent schools teachers are sometimes still called 'masters' and there is a range of additional pastoral roles to reflect the fact that many students are resident on site as boarders.

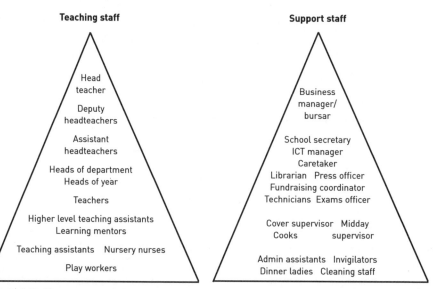

Figure 1 Staffing structure in UK schools. Note: see page 30 for an explanation of the support staff roles.

Overseeing everything are **governors**: volunteers who play a vital role guiding the work of the school at a senior level. The governors are led by the chair of governors. In law it is a school's governors who are responsible for what happens in a school and they are able to make the ultimate decisions on who is hired and fired. In practice, however, governors hand over the day-to-day running of the school to the headteacher and his or her senior staff – the deputy headteachers, assistant headteachers and other members of the senior leadership (or management) team.

So as a teacher working in a school you're responsible to your headteacher, but ultimately to your school's governors. For this reason it's worth getting to know the governors, and you should be aware that they may observe you teach at some point.

FASCINATING FACTS

On the first Tuesday in May every year, America celebrates the work of the country's teachers by holding 'National Teacher Day'. Unfortunately, it is not a school holiday!

SPECIALIST ROLES

In addition to the roles outlined above, teachers in schools carry out a range of additional specialist tasks. Often these become jobs in themselves, or carry an additional salary bonus. For example:

- special educational needs co-ordinator

- gifted and talented co-ordinator

- advanced skills teachers (who work in other schools as well as their own)

- pastoral co-ordinator (head of year, house).

Other staff support a range of schools in the teaching of specialist areas such as music and drama – so-called peripatetic teachers (see the interview on page 53).

MOVING INTO ADVISORY WORK

'Following eight years as a teacher and four as a successful head of geography, I felt the need to step back from the hectic pace of life in schools. I had organised a range of innovative projects whilst a teacher, several of which had won awards, and wanted to have the chance to work with a range of like-minded colleagues in different schools. I was looking for a role that combined the organising of creative education projects with an advisory capacity. I was also keen to study for a PhD in education to develop my interest in the psychology of learning, so began looking for a part-time advisory role that would enable me to do this.

'The role of Gifted and Talented Co-ordinator for a nearby local education authority caught my eye in the *Times Educational Supplement*. It involved advising and supporting the work of 14 secondary schools which had been given a budget to improve education for more able students. What excited me most was the opportunity to set up some really unusual projects which had never previously taken place in the area. As the role was part time (two and a half days a week), this gave me the chance to pursue my other interests.

'I was delighted to be offered the job following a successful interview and soon settled into the School Effectiveness Team, as my new department was called. The atmosphere was very different from a school, and it was great to be able to work with so many different teachers in contrasting schools. The fact that I had a substantial budget to work with that came as part of the government's Excellence in Cities initiative also made a big difference.

'One of the most exciting projects I organised was a real-life environmental problem-solving exercise in conjunction with our local business and enterprise partnership. Teams from each school had to put forward suggestions for how to solve the waste disposal problems of a major manufacturing firm. These were finally presented at a high-profile evening in the town centre, attended by the director of education, headteachers and the students' parents. The standard of work

> produced on that night has never been matched in my
> teaching career and in the words of one teacher, "the evening
> lifted the spirits of the town". I realised that a career in the
> advisory sector has a great deal to offer.'
>
> Jarvis Hayes, gifted and talented co-ordinator, Leeds

It should be noted that jobs such as exams officer and staff cover
co-ordinator, which were previously carried out by teachers, are
now being taken on by school support staff as the remodeling of the
school workforce gathers pace. The aim is that teachers should only
carry out teaching duties, or activities directly related to teaching
and learning (e.g. subject leader, manager of teaching and
learning).

CHAPTER 2

What is teaching really like?

There are no prizes for guessing that the bulk of a teacher's work involves standing in front of their classes helping children or young people learn. But there's much more to the role than that. A teacher is also required to perform a wide range of other tasks that complement the teaching of lessons, or otherwise help students to make academic and personal progress. These duties include:

- preparing lessons

- marking work

- setting and marking tests and mock exams

- keeping careful records of students' achievements and progress

- being a form tutor to a class

- attending staff meetings

- preparing for and attending parents' days or evenings

- carrying out duties at break and dinner

- getting involved in special projects outside the main curriculum.

In recent years there's been a big increase in the amount of paperwork and administration that teachers have to do. Though the government has made a commitment to reduce this administrative burden, many newly qualified teachers are still surprised by how much of their time is taken up by non-teaching activities.

'I went into teaching thinking that I would love it and I did – but it was the **teaching** I loved, not the paperwork, targets and problem behaviour. I'm now having second thoughts as to whether this is really a career for me.'

Jenny South, first year teacher, Southampton

DAVID READMAN, NEWLY QUALIFIED TEACHER
What is your role in education?
'I am in my first year of teaching. My timetable is 50% geography and 50% PE teaching in a secondary school.'

What is a typical day like?
'I get into school for about 7.30am and plan lessons for the day. I teach two lessons before break; they could be Geography in the classroom or PE outside. At break I usually have a meeting with one of the sports teams to check they are ready for their fixtures or I may be on break duty. There are another two lessons to teach before lunch when I either have sports practices with school teams or inter-house events to referee. As an NQT I have a free lesson per day, which equates to 50 minutes. This is often straight after lunch so I tend to eat my lunch in this time whilst doing any marking, admin, or ringing home about students that needs to be done. This time soon goes and then it's back to teaching last lesson. School finishes at 3.20pm. On a Monday there is always a meeting like a full staff meeting or departmental

meeting. The other four days are fixtures against other schools – league games or cup matches. I am usually home for about 6.30pm. Depending on the amount of work I have I will either stay in and do that, go to the gym or go training. Some nights I can easily work till 11pm, while other nights I don't bring much work home.'

When did you first become interested in teaching?
'Both my parents are teachers and seeing how hard they worked made me not want to go down this route. However, after graduating I wasn't really sure what to do. I worked on summer camps and did a lot of sports coaching. I then decided that perhaps being a PE teacher would actually be a good option.'

What hours do you work on an average week?
'Between 45 and 55 hours depending on how many fixtures I do.'

What qualifications do you have?
'A BSc (Hons) in Sport Science and Geography. I did the GTP course to qualify as a teacher and I have loads of coaching qualifications in many sports.'

What advice would you give somebody interested in pursuing a career in this field?
'Decide carefully on what route of training is best for you and your situation and then just go for it! Teaching PE is great, particularly in the summer: being outside, being with kids. However, be aware of all the marking, planning, paperwork and work you have to do at home.'

What are the highs and the lows of the job?
'The highs are being around young people, working outside, having long holidays and, for the GTP route, getting paid whilst you train. The lows are the long hours, dealing with the attitude of some students, and the amount of extra work you have to do.'

What could a job like yours lead on to?
'Lots of things, I'm sure, but with this being my first year I haven't really thought about it.'

The daily schedule of a teacher, whether they work in a primary or secondary school, follows a familiar routine (see table). In nursery schools children focus more on structured play throughout the day, and might attend for only a morning or afternoon session.

	MAIN ACTIVITIES
Before school starts	Most teachers arrive at school. Classrooms are prepared for the day; equipment is laid out. There's often a mad scramble for the photocopier as teachers get papers ready for the day. A formal briefing led by the headteacher usually starts the day, addressing key issues and passing on important news.
Registration	Teachers take the register with their classes, pass on important notices to students and collect in absence notes etc. Assemblies are often held during registration.
1st teaching session	The teaching day usually starts with two lessons. In primary schools these are normally taught by the class teacher (who takes their class for nearly all lessons); in secondary schools they're normally taught by specialist teachers.
Mid-morning break ('playtime')	In both primary and secondary schools there's usually a break from learning mid-morning. In primary schools this tends to be used by the children to run around and make as much noise as they can! In secondary schools things tend to be a bit more relaxed, with students often having a snack from the canteen. Teachers often don't get much time to switch off from lessons during break because they're busy collecting in materials or setting up things for the lessons that follow. Sometimes teachers will be required to do a break duty – supervising children's behaviour around the premises – often taking a coffee round with them as they circulate.

2nd teaching session	Another two lessons usually follow break.
Lunchtime	Obviously this is the time when the children stock up on food and drink, nowadays thankfully of a more healthy nature than in the past. Teachers also usually get some 'down time' during the lunch break to eat, reflect on the morning and make plans for the afternoon. If you're a PE or music teacher you may find yourself running clubs most lunchtimes.
3rd teaching session	After lunch another two lessons usually take place (in primary schools they are usually separated by another playtime).
After school	When the children have gone home is a time for meetings with all staff, or other teachers who teach children of the age group of your class (primary) or the same subject as you (secondary). Many teachers also use this time to tidy up their classrooms or catch up with marking. After-school parents' evenings (often ending quite late) have traditionally been a regular feature of teachers' lives, though in recent years there's been a growing trend to hold these briefings during the day. PE/music teachers often run after-school sports clubs, and this is also a time for other extra-curricular activities organised by teachers (e.g. the school play, Duke of Edinburgh Award scheme etc.).
At home	Most teachers take home a fair amount of work each night, and they usually spend at least half a day at the weekend working as well. Teachers' 'homework' usually consists of planning lessons and marking work, and many are still working late into the night.

Note that the daily schedule can be quite different in independent schools, where there are additional pastoral responsibilities and often extended hours. Many independent schools run sports activities one afternoon a week, but staff have to teach on Saturday mornings.

FASCINATING FACTS

The Gardening Club at Writhlington High School, near Bath, is not your average few seedlings and tomato plants affair. They grow rare orchids in the school labs and greenhouses and then send some of them to India to help save species from extinction. They've also exhibited at major flower shows, including Chelsea 2006.

SIÂN DOVER, HEAD OF DEPARTMENT
What is your role in education?
'I currently share the role of head of the PE department but I also teach GCSE Leisure and Tourism, Religious Studies and Physical Education.'

When did you first become interested in teaching?
'My mother was a teacher so I guess it is in the blood. I always wanted to be a teacher from a very young age but it was primary that I wanted to go into. I didn't really consider secondary until I actually came to apply for a teacher training course and a former PE teacher of mine said I would get more out of teaching PE to older students.'

What qualifications/training do you have?
'I have an upper second class honours degree in Physical Education and Geography and a PGCE in Secondary Physical Education. I also have coaching qualifications for virtually all the national curriculum activities taught by a PE teacher. I am also doing the Certificate in Primary Education conversion course as a night class.'

What is a typical day like?
'I work three days a week. I begin by dropping my two young children off at a day nursery at 7.30am. I get to school for about 8.20 in time for a morning staff briefing. After registering my year 11 form I go to teach lessons one and two before break. Depending on the day these are either classroom lessons, such as Leisure and Tourism, or practical

PE lessons. Mid-morning, we have a 25-minute break which enables me to have meetings with school sports teams and check their availability for coming fixtures and I sometimes manage to squeeze in a cup of tea. There are a further two lessons to teach before lunch, which again with a lot of subjects to teach could be either inside or out. Lunch lasts for an hour. I whizz down to the canteen at the start of the lunch break to get my free dinner, which I am entitled to because I do lunchtime clubs for students. It's then straight out to the courts or field to run the club where I eat my lunch whilst coaching or umpiring. I get back into school ready for the start of lesson five. I teach a further two lessons before the end of school at 3.15pm. At this time I either have a meeting or run a sport fixture. If the fixture is at home then it is usually finished by 5pm. If it is away then it can often be approaching 6pm by the time we get back to school. I then drive home and collect my children from nursery (if my husband hasn't already done so). After a couple of hours with my family I will usually start work on planning, marking, admin for the head of department role or writing reports. This can usually take me up to about 10.30pm.'

What hours do you work in an average week?
'I work part-time, three days a week (0.6 full-time equivalent). I do, however, work on some of the evenings that I don't go into school. I suppose it's between about 30 and 40 hours a week.'

What advice would you give somebody interested in pursuing a career in this field?
'Make sure you have lots of stamina, don't mind being on your feet all day and a strong bladder because you sometimes don't get chance to go to the toilet till the end of the day! It's very difficult being a working mother and you have to be organised, committed and willing to ask for help from family. You also need to get over the "guilt thing" of putting your children in nursery whilst you go out to work.'

What are the highs and lows of the job?
'The highs are helping your students pass their exams and being in contact with young people who have fresh new ideas. The holidays are also a bonus with a young family although they are very much needed and I still work throughout them. As a second income the money is reasonably good. The lows are the battles with discipline and the attitude of some students who don't want to learn and seem to lack respect for staff. The long hours and constant feeling that you just can't fit everything into the day is also frustrating. But I think the worst thing has to be how much work I have to do at home on an evening and therefore seem to have very little leisure time at all.'

What could a job like yours lead to?
'From a PE teacher or head of department you could go on to be a school sports co-ordinator (working across several schools) or a partnership development manager. You may also work up through the pastoral side or go on to become a deputy head. It could also lead to consultancy work and educational writing depending on the route you wanted to follow.'

CHANGING TIMES FOR TEACHERS

Classroom teachers form the bulk of the workforce in schools. In recent years, however, a range of new support roles has developed to help enhance education for children and young people, including learning mentors, specialist teaching assistants and IT managers. The government has tried to place greater emphasis on the classroom role of the teacher by gradually removing non-teaching duties as part of a re-modelling of the profession.

SCHOOL SUPPORT STAFF

The following staff work alongside teachers to provide a safe, efficient and effective school.

STUDENT SUPPORT

Teaching assistants usually work with a teacher in their classroom, making sure students get the most out of lessons (e.g. by helping them find their way around a computer).

Higher-level teaching assistants usually undertake more complex tasks and tend to work more independently than other classroom-based staff.

Nursery nurses – specialists who look after the social and educational development of children up to the age of eight years old.

Play workers plan, organise and supervise play and activities for children and young people inside and outside school.

Learning mentors work with school and college students to help them address barriers (and potential barriers) to learning through supportive one-to-one relationships and sometimes small group work.

Cover supervisors – suitably trained school staff who supervise students by carrying out pre-prepared exercises when teaching staff are on short-term absence.

Midday supervisors, sometimes called lunchtime supervisors or lunchtime assistants, look after the welfare of school students during lunchtimes.

ADMINISTRATION

Bursars, sometimes called school business managers or senior administrators, play a crucial strategic role in schools, making the most of the available resources to ensure teaching and learning get the financial support they need.

Library staff manage all the print, online and e-learning resources that are available in the modern school library, so that students and teachers can access all the materials they need to help them learn and teach.

Admin assistants provide vital office support, from answering phones to ordering stationery, entering data on computers and filing paperwork.

Secretaries play a crucial role in the day-to-day life of a school by providing a wide range of administrative support to keep everything running as smoothly as possible.

Invigilators assist with the administration of exams.

Press officers help to promote a positive image of the school.

Fundraising co-ordinators help to raise money for the school.

TECHNICIANS

Science – play a vital role in the provision of high-quality science teaching in schools, from looking after laboratory equipment to helping students achieve their potential with one-to-one support.

ICT – have an increasingly important role in schools, as teaching and learning become more and more dependent on new technology.

Design and technology – help make sure teachers and students can get the most out of D&T lessons.

Food – help ensure food technology lessons run smoothly and efficiently.

Sports – help students get the most out of sports and PE activities in schools.

SITE STAFF

Cleaning staff ensure classrooms, corridors, halls and toilets are kept clean and hygienic, working on their own or as part of a team, depending on the size of the school.

Catering staff – catering staff or kitchen assistants help provide nutritious, balanced and value-for-money meals to children every lunchtime under the direction of the head cook or catering manager.

Cooks provide nutritious, balanced and value-for-money meals to children every lunchtime in term time.

Premises managers/caretakers play a vital role in schools by taking over the management of frontline caretaking, cleaning and security from teachers.

FASCINATING FACTS

From September 2006 schools will receive 50p per head (primary schools) and 60p per head (secondary schools) to provide healthy, nutritionally balanced school lunches. In prisons 60p per head is spent on providing lunch; prior to the new guidelines this was double the average amount spent in primary schools.

Teachers and school managers have generally welcomed the greater emphasis on the teacher's role as teacher, but at the same time increasing demands have been placed on school support staff. The recent move to set aside planning, preparation and assessment (PPA) time for teachers in all state schools has been part of this transition.

There is a host of additional support roles for teachers: local education authority advisers, specialist teachers and external consultants who provide additional training and guidance to help teachers improve. These are career options for experienced teachers looking to work with teachers to help them improve their work.

HELPING SCHOOLS BECOME MORE EFFECTIVE
'My role as an education consultant takes me throughout the country as I support the work of teachers and school managers. Rather than somebody who pretends they have all the answers, I try to ask probing questions that help people to see what the most appropriate next step is for them. As we talk, many teachers realise that they have not paused to think deeply about their work for quite some time. I use my experience and expertise to reassure the people I work with that the ideas they have are perfectly valid – in many cases what they need is reassurance from somebody whose judgement they trust. I also try to suggest things that encourage them to see their situation more creatively.

'I've been lucky to have been asked to write a range of books for teachers, including several titles in the award-winning

Teachers' Pocketbooks, which are handy sized but serious summaries of key issues in education. It's always a thrill to see your book on the shelves in places like Waterstone's, and even better when people write to you and tell you how useful they've found your work. Having had some success writing, I now also get asked to advise publishers on education books. I attend events such as the Education Show in order to meet potential readers and learn about the latest products.

'Most months I'm involved in a fair amount of training work with teachers and more recently with headteachers too. It's very rewarding but very challenging work. While some of the people I train are ready for change, others are confused about what to do next, and some not sure that they want to change! It's sometimes like working with those reluctant students at the back of the class who sit with their arms folded – perhaps the teachers have been taking lessons from these students?

'Although my work as an education consultant seems far removed from my previous career as a teacher, I think I share the same mission – to improve educational opportunities for young people in our schools. Although the pay and holidays are not as attractive as if I'd stayed in schools, I am much more flexible and I love being my own boss. This year I am off to Italy in June to go trekking among the spring wild flowers of the Dolomites, something I could never have done as a teacher.'

Brin Best, education consultant, Otley

THE FORMAL AND INFORMAL CURRICULUM

Whether teaching in England, Scotland, Wales or Northern Ireland, teachers in the state sector work within the framework of the **national curriculum** (see box). Independent schools, however, do not have to cover the national curriculum.

The national curriculum is a document that sets out the knowledge, understanding and skills expected of children and young people at different stages in their schooling. The English national curriculum covers 12 subject areas:

- English

- Maths

- Science

- Design and Technology

- Information and Communication Technology

- History

- Geography

- Modern Foreign Languages

- Art and Design

- Music

- Physical Education

- Citizenship.

The national curriculum has a major influence – some would say an overbearing one – on the day-to-day work of teachers. While most teachers welcomed its introduction in the late 1980s, some have found it too prescriptive and detailed. For these teachers it seems that flexibility, fun and creativity are disappearing from schools.

FASCINATING FACTS

When Xaverian Sixth Form College in Manchester couldn't find a film version of the play The Trojan Women for their A level Theatre Studies project, they solved the problem by making their own version and releasing it on DVD.

Teachers also oversee what has been called the 'informal' or 'hidden' curriculum. This encompasses the wider personal and life skills of children and young people, including their ability to get on with others and develop a sense of responsibility. In short, this hidden curriculum is about preparing young people for life in the society in which they'll live. Though not written down by the government, the importance of this alternative curriculum is recognised by everyone. Now that citizenship – education about society and about children's rights and responsibilities within society – is embedded as a national curriculum subject, there are clearer links between the national and the so-called hidden curriculum.

'I was a Sikh in a Catholic school; the only boy in a turban. Ronnie made a difficult (as difficult as a middle-class upbringing in the west of Scotland gets) time in my life much easier. What I remember most was his teaching Robert Bolt's *A Man for All Seasons*. I was inspired to go off to study law because of that book.'

Hardeep Singh Kohli, writer and comedian

GOVERNMENT INITIATIVES

Another important factor affecting the work of teachers is the range of government initiatives that have been introduced recently. These are intended to tackle key priorities or areas of underachievement in education and they mirror some of the reforms that have taken place in modernising other public services, such as the health service.

Both the national curriculum and the recent government initiatives have brought with them considerable additional paperwork and administration for schools. Much of the burden of this work has fallen on teachers, which has led to frustration and accusations of 'initiative overload'. Information about all the latest government initiatives can be found at www.teachernet.gov.uk.

RECENT GOVERNMENT EDUCATION INITIATIVES
Here is a selection of the many education initiatives now under way in schools in the UK.

England and Wales

- Assessment for Learning

- Behaviour Improvement Programme

- Circle Time

- Ethnic Minority and Vulnerable Children Achievement

- Excellence in Cities

- Extended Day

- Gender and Achievement

- Gifted and Talented

- Healthy Schools Initiative

- ICT Across the Curriculum

- Leading Edge Partnership Programme

- Literacy and Numeracy Strategies and Summer Schools

- Playing for Success

- School Workforce Remodelling

- Sure Start

- School Diversity Programme

- Thinking Skills.

Scotland

- Curriculum for Excellence

- Assessment is for Learning

- Determined to Succeed (enterprise initiative)

- Education for Citizenship

- Future Learning and Teaching Programme (FLAT)

- Health Promoting Schools.

Northern Ireland

- Reinvestment and Reform

- Public Private Partnerships

- Key Stage 4 Flexibility Initiative

- Good Practice Initiative.

FASCINATING FACTS

In 2004 there were 49,544 teachers in Scotland. The average age of teachers in Scotland is 44.

Working in schools means getting used to the fact that things do work in cycles and that change is an inevitable part of the system. A thorough review of the national curriculum is now on the horizon, which could have further far-reaching implications for teachers.

EXTENDED SCHOOLS
One of the most important new initiatives that will shape schools over the coming years is called 'extended schools'. The government's vision is that schools will open their doors to lifelong learning, community projects and child care all day and into the evening, as well as being open in the holidays. This will be in addition to their main role as providers of education to school-age children.

Although some schools already run community education programmes, extended schools will take this much further by making schools the hub of their communities, offering a whole host of services that are currently beyond their scope. The challenge is that by 2010 all schools will provide a suite of new services called the 'core offer', with some going much further. Although not all these new activities are expected to be organised and run by teachers, anybody planning to go into teaching in the next few years is bound to see the influence of the extended schools initiative. If everything goes to plan it's set to change the way we see schools forever, and make them an even more important part of all our communities.

WHAT DOES THIS MEAN?
So what does all this mean if you're considering a career in teaching? Well, if you're somebody who enjoys flexibility, independence and the opportunity to think outside the box then teaching (in a state school at least) might soon seem like a rather frustrating career choice. It's worth sticking at it, however, as there is still a place for creativity in teaching today. Indeed, without creative teachers schools would be incredibly boring places in which to be a student! It's just worth bearing in mind that the government does not always provide the ideal conditions for creativity to shine through. At times ministers can seem too worried by tests and targets to care about the role of fun in learning. The challenge is to strike a professional balance between wanting to express your independence as a qualified teacher for the benefit of your students, and delivering the many strands of the government's reforms.

HOW MUCH DO TEACHERS EARN?

In the past teaching was not valued as much as it is today and salaries in this country were quite low. A series of strikes and other industrial action in the 1980s helped to boost teacher salaries, with the result that teaching became a much more financially rewarding profession. Teaching is now generally recognised as a fairly well-paid job compared to many of the alternatives for graduates, especially for jobs in the so-called public sector (e.g. health, other local authority work). If you progress into management, salaries of more than £50,000 are on offer and the top headteachers earn over £90,000 a year.

It's also worth noting that teachers in the UK earn some of the highest teachers' salaries in the world, so some countries have clearly to catch up when it comes to valuing their teachers. This needs to be borne in mind if you're considering teaching abroad.

KAREN BROOM, DEPUTY HEADTEACHER, INTERNATIONAL SCHOOL, ITALY
What is your role in education?
'I'm a deputy head and class teacher at a small English international school in Rosa, northern Italy. The majority of children attending are Italian but all of the lessons (except Italian!) are held in English. I'm responsible for the co-ordination of the English curriculum and staff. This involves searching for teachers currently based in England and enrolling them in the school, and liaison between the English and Italian staff.'

Why did you decide to work in this particular area of education?
'I was keen to teach abroad because I had taught in the UK for a while and wanted a break from the heavy workload and large class sizes in the UK. I also wanted experience of living abroad, experiencing a different culture and climate. My move into deputy headship was stimulated by my desire to gain more responsibility without returning to the UK.'

What qualifications/training do you have that are relevant to the role?

'I have a BSc in biological sciences and a PGCE. I have no specific training or qualification for my co-ordination role. My many years of experience as a class teacher of a range of ages in international schools in northern Italy have prepared me well for my current role.'

What particular skills are necessary for your job?

'Knowledge of the UK and Italian school curricula is essential, as is an insight into both the British and Italian education systems. Good spoken Italian is also paramount. For my co-ordination role experience of living and working in Italy and knowledge of such things as contracts is also useful. It's vital to be flexible and patient as getting things done can be very frustrating in Italy! Good people skills are important when it comes to interviewing new staff and giving emotional support to new (and homesick!) teachers. Organisational skills are also really important, as there's so much to get through in the day.'

Describe a typical day

'I arrive at school just after 8am and check staff absences, arranging cover as necessary. Then I check emails if we're carrying out a staff search, and check the organisation of the day, relaying any information to teachers. I then get things ready in my classroom for the teaching day. I teach from 8.45 until 10.30am, when there's a mid-morning break, during which I might liaise with the directors of the school (one of whom is the headteacher) or other members of staff, depending on the burning issues of the day. I then teach again from 11am until 1pm, which is lunchtime, when I get on with more administrative duties such as computer tasks, making phone calls, or liaison with other staff. From 2.30pm onwards I might teach again, or have a non-contact period for my deputy headship duties. At 4pm the children go home, and I might speak to parents if necessary or meet with some teachers. I then start preparing lessons for the next day, or putting up displays of children's work. I also carry out more co-ordination work such as ordering resources, organising the book club or staff recruitment. I usually go home about 6pm.'

What are working conditions like in your job?
'The official hours are 8.30am to 4.10pm Monday to Friday, with a 30-minute break mid-morning and 90 minutes for lunch. There are 14–15 weeks holiday a year for teachers and very little additional work to do in the holidays – this is a bonus compared to the UK. Italian contract conditions are good in terms of sick pay, maternity leave etc. but wages are generally much lower than the UK.'

What are the highs and lows of the job?
'There are many highs. Working with children every day is different – you're never bored. I get much satisfaction from seeing children learn and develop under my care. The small class sizes in my school mean that I feel like I'm really teaching something. Meeting different people and experiencing new cultures is also very interesting. On the negative side teaching in an international school is still stressful and draining, just like in the UK. The lack of organisation in Italy (a national characteristic!) can be frustrating, especially where children are involved.'

What advice would you give somebody who is interested in pursuing a career in this field?
'Get teaching experience in the UK first, as in my experience there's very little support for new teachers abroad. Research the schools and country well. For example, European contracts and conditions are not the same as in the UK and there could be nasty surprises down the line. Speak to someone who has done it, as they will have the inside information you need. I would say that it's definitely a good experience, but don't expect to make millions!'

What could a job like this lead on to?
'The next step would be a head of an international school. You might also consider opening your own English international school.'

SALARIES FOR TEACHERS IN ENGLAND AND WALES (STATE SECTOR)

TEACHING ASSISTANTS
Salaries are set locally but usually range between £12,400 and £13,900.

JAYNE LODGE, TEACHING ASSISTANT (SECONDARY)
What is your role in education?
'A teaching assistant attached to the science department.'

What is a typical day like?
'Assisting the lower-ability students to access the work set by the teacher.'

When did you first become interested in working in education?
'I assisted in some voluntary work at school and really enjoyed it, particularly working with the students.'

What hours do you work in an average week?
'25 hours.'

What qualifications/training do you have?
'O levels, CSEs, EAL (English as an Additional Language), adult numeracy and literacy, Dealing with Misconceptions in Chemistry, Physics and Biology, NVQ level 2.'

What advice would you give to somebody interested in pursuing a career in this field?
'You would need to be very flexible and enjoy working with children. You need a wide variety of interpersonal skills.'

What are the highs and lows of the job?
'The good things about the job are working with the students, assisting in their learning. The bad things are too many students and not enough time.'

What could a job like yours lead on to?
'Further training to higher-level teaching assistant. You could also go on to do teacher training.'

UNQUALIFIED TEACHERS

Unqualified teachers, such as instructors, are paid on a ten-point scale ranging from £14,391 to £22,761. The governing body decides where on the scale an unqualified teacher should start, and may also pay an additional allowance on top of this. Trainee teachers following the employment-based route (see pages 69–71) may be paid on the qualified or unqualified teachers' pay scale.

SUPPLY TEACHERS

Teachers on short-term contracts with a school or local education authority are, for most purposes, treated and expected to act as regular teachers. They are covered by the School Teachers' Pay and Conditions Document and are a paid a salary in the usual way. However, a supply teacher employed through a teacher employment agency is not an employee of the school or of the local authority. Such teachers are not entitled to the rates of pay set out in the School Teachers' Pay and Conditions Act, but have the same duties and obligations as any other teacher. This is determined by the supply agency they work for.

CLASSROOM TEACHERS

They start on the main pay scale, usually on point M1, but if they have other teaching experience they may start higher up the scale. Schools may also award discretionary points for relevant experience. Teachers get a salary rise every time the pay scales and allowances are uprated. Each September, teachers on the main pay scale move to the next point up the scale, subject to satisfactory performance, but they may advance by two points if their performance is excellent. Qualified teachers who reach the top of the main pay scale can apply to be assessed against eight national standards to cross the 'threshold' to the upper pay scale. This provides an opportunity for good classroom teachers to progress to a higher salary range. To date around 95% of teachers who apply are successful.

CATEGORY	PAY* SEPT 2006
Newly Qualified Teacher	£19,641
Qualified teacher (six years experience)	£28,707
Qualified teacher (top of upper pay scale)	£33,444

* As at September 2006. Note that additional allowances are payable in each category for London and the London fringe.

Additional payments – teaching and learning responsibility (TLR) payments – can boost teachers' basic salary. These are payable when a member of staff performs duties that exceed those of a normal classroom teacher, for example duties that:

● require a teacher to use additional professional skills and judgement

● require him/her to lead and manage student development across the curriculum

● have an impact on the progress of students other than those in the teacher's assigned classes or groups of students

● involve leading, developing and enhancing the teaching of other staff.

There are two levels of allowance: TLR2 and TLR1. To qualify for the latter, the teacher must also manage a significant number of staff. Many heads of department in secondary schools and subject coordinators in primary schools are give TLR payments.

ALLOWANCE	AMOUNT PAYABLE
TLR2 TLR1	£2,306–5,689 £6,663–11,275

Classroom teachers who take on special educational needs responsibilities can receive additional payments of between £1,818 and £3,597.

ADVANCED SKILLS TEACHERS (ASTS)
These are teachers who work both in their own schools and also more widely with a range of partner schools, sharing good practice and improving teaching and learning. They have their own pay spine, which ranges from £34,083 to £51,819. Each AST is paid within a five-point range based primarily on the nature of their work, the scale of the challenges to be tackled, the professional competencies needed and any other recruitment considerations. ASTs get an

increase in salary when the pay scales are uprated and may also be awarded extra points each September for high-quality performance. The AST grade offers excellent classroom teachers the chance to continue teaching (rather than progressing into management) and use their skills to enhance the performance of other teachers. The generous pay spine reflects the fact that the grade is an alternative career path to taking up a leadership or management post.

EXCELLENT TEACHERS

The new Excellent Teacher Scheme (ETS) allows schools to create posts for teachers that gives them a clear role in the school, but, unlike ASTs, they have no outreach function in other schools. The first Excellent Teacher appointments will be made in September 2006 after applications are assessed against Excellent Teacher Standards. The starting salary will be £35,874.

LEADERSHIP GROUP

School leaders (including assistant heads, deputy heads and headteachers) are paid on the 43-point leadership spine, which extends from £34,083 to £95,631. Headteachers' pay is normally related to school size, but schools can pay more where necessary to recruit and retain headteachers in challenging schools. The headteacher's pay will also reflect the type of school he or she works in, with secondary heads being paid more than primary heads. Deputies and assistant heads are paid on a five-point range below that of the headteacher and above the pay of the highest-paid classroom teacher. Members of the Leadership Group all receive an increase when the pay scales are uprated, but may also be awarded one or two pay points in September each year, provided their performance is of high quality.

TREVOR WEAR, HEADTEACHER
What is your role in education?
'I am the headteacher of a medium-sized secondary school in the Yorkshire Dales. My role is actually called "principal" as my school is a specialist technology college. I see my role as a guardian of the ethos of the school.'

When did you first become interested in teaching?
'As a research engineer in the nuclear industry (age 27).'

What qualifications/training do you have?
'An upper second class honours degree, a PGCE in Physics and Maths and an unfinished PhD!'

What is a typical day like?
'I arrive in school at 7.50am and open my emails and do any urgent admin tasks. At 8.20 I go down to lead the staff briefing. Between 8.30 and 12.30 a typical day usually consists of two hours' administration, one hour meeting and one hour teaching. Then 12.30 to 1.30pm is lunchtime. I do a 15-minute supervision at the start of the lunch break and 10 minutes at the end, leaving about 35 minutes for lunch. From 1.30 to 3.15, the end of the teaching day, I do an hour's admin and usually spend the rest of the time in meetings. I always have a school-related meeting between 3.30 and 4.30 and then go home for a couple of hours break. Between 6.30 and 9.00pm is spent planning, doing admin or attending evening meetings.'

What hours do you work in an average week?
'It's very difficult to say. Does thinking count? It's probably between 60 and 70 hours per week in term time.'

What advice would you give to somebody interested in pursuing a career in this field?
'Ask yourself if you genuinely like young people. Be very good at organising your time and working under pressure ... it can be very rewarding.'

What are the highs and lows of the job?
'The highs are when you succeed with a challenging student and when things work or fall into place. The lows are the persistent political meddling and the politicisation of education.'

What could a job like yours lead on to?
'A nervous breakdown! No, seriously consultancy work or writing.'

SCOTTISH PAY BANDS

The pay banding system is different in Scotland, as is progression in teaching. The following table gives a simplified outline of pay awards.

CATEGORY	PAY RATE*
Probationer teacher (NQT equivalent)	£19,440
Teacher with one year's experience	£23,316
Teacher with six years' experience	£31,008
Chartered teacher (equivalent to upper pay scale in England)	£31,968–38,013
Principal teacher (e.g. with subject responsibility)	£33,804–43,635
Assistant heads and headteachers (secondary schools are generally smaller than in England and Wales, so the upper pay range is not as high)	£38,343–74,844

* As at April 2006.

NORTHERN IRISH PAY BANDS

The pay banding system is different in Northern Ireland, as is progression in teaching. The following table gives a simplified outline of pay awards.

CATEGORY	PAY RATE*
Probationer teacher (NQT equivalent)	£19,161
Teacher with six years' experience	£28,005
Upper pay scale	£30,339–£32,628
Leadership group (subject responsibility/ pastoral responsibility or management) – including assistant heads and deputy heads	£33,249–£88,797 (this is a 41 point scale)
Principals (heads)	£37,617–£88,797

* As at September 2005.

Unqualified teachers are paid at a set hourly rate ranging between £13.12 and £16.92, depending on the specific nature of their duties.

Note: salaries in the independent sector can vary widely, but many independent schools strive to pay above the rate a teacher or school manager would be paid in a similarly-sized state school.

'The thing about Mr Moles was that he used to make himself laugh. He always stood to read, and he would slowly slide down the side of his big table and sometimes end up on the floor in laughter. I was often unable to stand up at the end because my legs were so weak from laughing. That has been my benchmark for laughter ever since.'

Sue Townsend, best-selling author

THE INDEPENDENT SECTOR

Newly qualified teachers (NQTs) can only complete their induction in independent schools that meet certain national curriculum requirements. There is no legal requirement, however, for independent schools to offer induction.

In 1999 the Independent Schools' Council Teacher Induction Panel was established to provide statutory induction for NQTs wishing to teach in the independent sector. Satisfactory completion of induction does not confer any additional qualification or formal status on an NQT, but it does enable him or her to seek teaching posts in state schools and to register with the GTC in England or Wales. Without completing statutory induction teachers can still teach in the independent sector but cannot transfer to the state sector. Teachers other than NQTs moving to the independent sector may find that there is a requirement to complete a probationary period before employment is confirmed.

Independent schools set their own salary scales and are not obliged to follow those set out in the School Teachers' Pay and Conditions Document. Consequently, terms and conditions of service will vary throughout the independent sector, depending on school size, location and type. Many independent schools have a longer working day, but the holidays are also significantly longer. The benefits made available to staff vary greatly, but may include the provision of free or subsidised accommodation (mainly but not exclusively in boarding schools), fee remission for their children's education, private medical insurance, access for the family to school facilities such as swimming pools, squash and tennis courts, and free meals. Often independent schools offer smaller class sizes and access to a wider range of facilities.

OTHER BENEFITS

Pay makes up only one aspect of any job's benefits – holidays, pension, day-to-day working conditions and the protection given to workers also need to be considered when weighing up the pros and cons of teaching as a career. On all these counts, teaching fares very well.

Teachers are the constant butt of jokes from their non-teaching friends about long holidays and short days. The truth, of course, is that many teachers work very long hours during term time (as the interviews in this book show), and often work into their holidays too. The idea that they drop everything as soon as the students go home is certainly a fantasy. Over the course of a year, however, the hours worked by teachers do tend to balance out and compare with the hours worked by most other people – it's just that term times tend to be very intense and the holidays more relaxed periods for teachers. If you're someone who finds intense work difficult to bear for long periods, then teaching is sure to help develop your stamina!

Teachers' day-to-day working conditions are hectic and demanding, but you get the chance to work with some very supportive colleagues and schools are usually clean and safe places in which to work. Although they often like to complain about their jobs, most teachers are actually happy with their working lives. The interviews in the book show time and time again that working with young people can be very rewarding.

FASCINATING FACTS

**A survey by the Teacher Support Network showed that
approximately 12% of teachers say they have been abused
or assaulted by parents.**

Teachers' pensions are among the best that are available, and as a
teacher you enjoy a level of job security that is unheard of in the
private sector, where people are often hired and fired because they
simply do not fit in. The popular TV programme *The Apprentice*
gives a glimpse of the ruthlessness of the business world. It is in
fact very hard to sack a teacher unless they've done something
seriously wrong. If you want it to be, teaching can still be one of the
few 'jobs for life' that remain in this country. To keep on top of the
job you will, however, need to be prepared to be a lifelong learner
yourself – no one is ever the finished article when it comes to
teaching.

Because there are so many teachers in the country (more than half
a million), the unions that represent teachers are very powerful and
work extremely hard to get a better deal for the profession. There's
also a lot of help on hand if you need individual support, or are
experiencing difficulties at work. This is certainly another benefit of
choosing teaching as a career.

CHAPTER 3

How do I get into teaching?

If you want to teach in a state school you must first obtain Qualified Teacher Status (QTS) and undergo a course of Initial Teacher Training (ITT). For your first year of employment you'll be known as a Newly Qualified Teacher (NQT) and you need to pass this induction year to be entitled to a permanent contract. All NQTs are given a mentor within their school, usually a fellow staff member, who is responsible for helping them have a successful induction year.

Gaining QTS does mean that you are entitled to work in either secondary or primary schools, but realistically you'll be more likely to be employed in a school from the stage you were trained in. It's possible to do a conversion course if you want to switch between the two and these are usually held as evening classes by some colleges and universities, to enable you to continue working in the day.

A CHANGE OF DIRECTION?
'I'd been working as a secondary PE teacher for nine years. I'd had my two children during this time and had gone back to work as the joint head of the department for three days a week.

'I travelled about 45 minutes each way to work and I began to feel that this extra one and a half hours in the day could be better used either by planning, marking, having sports fixtures or by spending time with my own children. I was also finding that the attitude of the students had changed over the past few years and that behaviour was getting harder to manage.

'I decided it was time for a change. I still wanted to work in education but wasn't sure what to do until someone mentioned to me about a conversion course to primary which was running at Bradford College. I decided that, if I did the course, then my options would be open as to whether I applied for another secondary job or a primary position. As there are more primary schools around I thought it may be an opportunity to find a job nearer to home and thus reduce travelling time per day.'

Emily Doyle, PE teacher, Ilkley

If you're keen to work in a specific area of education as a teacher (e.g. special educational needs), then it's necessary to gain QTS first (perhaps taking a course in your area of interest) and then work towards your specific career goal. If you want to work as a peripatetic music or drama teacher, then you need to have QTS if you want to be paid the higher rates – equivalent to the hourly rate of a music teacher.

HOWARD ROGERSON, PERIPATETIC MUSIC TEACHER
When did you first become interested in working in music education?
'I first went to music college at the age of 15 and even then knew that I wanted to get people to enjoy music as much as I do. I've always believed that teaching is performing and performing is teaching and that the two things should run parallel with one another. Throughout my professional career as a performer I've worked in schools and had the good fortune in 1983 to be involved in Shape up North – a project designed to involve artists in the community. This involved me

in developing music in the setting of a mental hospital and looking at music as another language by which we communicate. While working with Opera North I was involved extensively with education and so I've always found it to be a key element of my work.'

What is your role in education?
'I'm currently a full-time peripatetic teacher of woodwind in North Craven, Yorkshire. Unlike most peripatetic music teachers I work on a full-time contract. This means that I visit a range of different schools and age groups each week and work with small groups and individuals. I teach flute, oboe, clarinet, bassoon, saxophone and more recently fife (a small flute used in military music). This is a new venture as I'm encouraging younger students to take up fife as it provides skills needed for other instruments at a later stage, without them encountering some of the difficulties presented by other instruments – such as not having a large enough hand span to cover notes. In addition to this I work with Skipton Music Centre and direct the junior band and chamber ensemble and run a theory class at the centre. I also work with adults in Settle Orchestra and in schools work with year 2 students upwards.'

Why did you decide to work in this particular area?
'I was strongly influenced by my own teachers who inspired me by their work. I was thought not to be quite of the level for full performance standard and so undertook a performance and teaching course which covered both elements equally. This was a wonderfully designed course in that it gave a good grounding in a wide range of instruments, honed performance skills and also gave experience in teaching. We had to cover teaching not only of our own main instrument but also allied instruments, so we had to be very versatile and adaptable. I played the clarinet professionally but also took a teaching diploma and remained involved in education through tuition and work in education with Opera North. I also worked as an examiner for Leeds University and taught at both Leeds and Huddersfield University. I've also taught

clarinet for A level music in Harrogate and been involved in every age group from primary music through to university graduates. I also have some pensioner students. I began working as a peripatetic teacher in North Craven some 20 years ago on a part-time basis but gradually increased my commitment and then eventually accepted a full-time post.'

What qualifications/training do you have that are relevant to the role?
'I am a graduate of the Royal Northern College of Music and hold diplomas in both teaching and performance as an Associate of the Royal Northern College of Music, along with a teaching diploma as an Associate of the Royal College of Music in London. I also have an Open University degree in social science.'

What particular skills are necessary for this job?
'You need to enjoy your music and to like people. The job requires enthusiasm, patience and dedication. You also need exceptionally good communication skills and empathy to be able to put yourself in the role of the student when they're having difficulties and be able to examine their barriers to understanding and to find ways to explain things more effectively. This can sometimes mean that you have to try a lot of different approaches to find the one that works for that individual. You always need to be aware of the needs of the individual student. Being a peripatetic teacher involves you working closely with a number of schools and so you have to be versatile and aware of the needs of the schools. You're also working to raise the profile of the subject in schools and increase their awareness of how music relates to other areas of the curriculum. In practical terms you need to have a high standard of piano playing in order to accompany students and help them to reach a level of fuller development and understanding in aural work.'

What are the working conditions like in your job?
'These can vary dramatically. There are very few education authorities at present where full music services survive and

so there are not many specialists on full-time contracts. The majority of posts are sessional or pro rata. The normal teaching contract conditions apply and I work a standard week and also have planning, preparation and assessment time. This sometimes comes in the form of odd half-hours during the day but there is also some at the beginning and end of terms. There is also a commitment to working with the rest of the team to develop area strategies and to put together a playing week in which we work as performers in schools. However, my days vary considerably and some days I will work from 8am to 5pm rather than the standard school day. Sometimes sessions begin before school and other times they are scheduled after lessons end. Lunchtimes vary and I commute between schools, so school timetables do not always coincide. I can move between primary and secondary in one day or find myself in three to four different primaries in the course of a day. The actual teaching areas also vary dramatically depending on the size and layout of the school. I've even taught in a toilet block and corridor! Usually my timetable means that I have to cover a set number of students per hour but the range of ability and age is varied.'

What are the highs and lows of the job?

'The lows are to do with some of the restrictions. There's a lot of paperwork, with records for every student and individual development plans. There are also increasing regulations which can sometimes seem intrusive. An example of this is when dealing with child protection issues – this makes it difficult at times as you cannot touch a student and so if you are working on a one-to-one basis you can't move their fingers to show them how to cover a note. You also have to be aware of situations where you yourself might be vulnerable and ensure that you never stand between a student and a doorway, blocking their exit. You also sometimes find in schools that your subject is not given any kind of acknowledgement (e.g. the students' progress is not recognised), often because you're not seen as part of the school but as someone who comes in to the school. This can be frustrating when a student has worked hard and achieved good results. Another problem can be that if the subject is not valued it's difficult to follow up why a student might not attend sessions or occasionally staff don't release them for sessions. However, the real high point is being able to see students develop. This is not just about achieving certificates but actually helping each student to reach their own potential and seeing the effect which this can have on them in all areas of their life and personality. Music involves the use of the whole brain and can have hugely beneficial effects. It's also very rewarding to see students' growing involvement in the subject and to see them starting to work together.'

Describe a typical day
'There really is no such thing. However, each day does have a very tight schedule and involves seeing a wide range of students. Alongside the teaching there are also issues such as maintaining parental contacts, dealing with timetabling problems that arise, following up on missed sessions and dealing with other practical and emotional problems which can interfere with a student's performance. Generally attendance is very good but it's important to have a follow-up system to ensure that difficulties don't escalate. Parental liaison is vital as it's very important to balance costs with both parental and student expectations and provide a programme which encourages development. Structured courses are very important in order to retain enthusiasm.'

What advice would you give somebody who is interested in pursuing a career in this field?
'Sadly, the current system is undergoing a number of changes and the potential for a full-time career in this area is limited at present. The current trend to focus on academic-based expectations is currently stifling creative subjects in the curriculum. It is therefore important for musicians who wish to work in education to focus on acquiring a broad range of practical skills in order to help them to find work and develop their own talent and encourage creativity in others.'

What could a job like this lead on to?
'Opportunities for full-time work are limited, although there are posts in education organisation, such as head of music centres etc. The majority of posts are part-time and many peripatetic teachers will work for a number of education authorities.'

QTS is not necessarily needed to teach English as an Additional Language or in independent schools, sixth-form colleges, further education colleges or City Technology Colleges, but it is getting harder to find a job in these institutions if you don't have this teaching qualification.

Because of the need for more teachers the government has tried to increase the different routes through which you can gain QTS to enable all people who have the potential to become a good teacher to have the chance, regardless of their circumstances. This chapter looks at the many varied routes into teaching and the qualifications or experience needed in order to embark on each one.

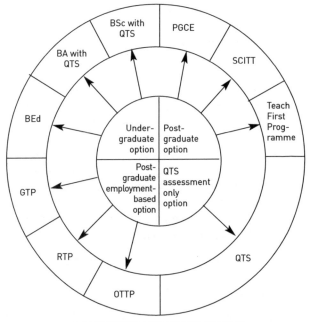

QUALIFICATIONS AND TRAINING COURSES

CHRISTOPHER CLARKE, TEACHING ENGLISH AS A FOREIGN LANGUAGE TUTOR

When did you first become interested in working in education?
'I first thought I might pursue a career in teaching TEFL when I was 30. My work as a TEFL teacher involves working with adults who speak another language who are trying to learn English'

Why did you decide to work in this particular area?
'I was offered a job in a language school in Cambridge and really enjoyed it, so I decided to do a TEFL to improve my ability to teach English'

What qualifications/ training do you have relevant to the role?
'I have a TEFL standard qualification.'

What particular skills are required for the job?
'There are a number of skills required for the job. These include creativity, patience and the ability to make complicated things simple. It also helps to be sociable. The job also involves teamwork but you must also be able to work independently using your own initiative.'

Describe a typical day
'This varies from week to week but you would start at 9am and do up to five hours' teaching. You then use the breaks and the afternoon to plan the next lessons. Sometimes this means I don't get home until 5 or 6pm.'

What are working conditions like?
'When there's a lot of work, the days are busy and there's not often a chance to sit down and relax! Otherwise there might not be much to do and of course you don't get paid. It's not very satisfying as the work is very seasonal; either you're extremely busy or you don't have enough to do. In my particular situation I don't feel very valued by the school.'

What are the highs and lows?
'Low morale amongst staff, contraction of the TEFL industry (at least in the UK), low pay, irregular hours. The highs are

you can travel all over the world and teach. Also you get to meet many people from all over the world. On the downside, it is difficult to get a permanent job in the UK.'

What advice would you give somebody interested in pursuing a career in this field?
'Have another job on the side that you can do during the quiet periods, e.g. web design or writing.'

What could a job like this lead on to?
'TEFL is a bit of a dead end. You can end up managing a language school or get to be a producer of TEFL teaching material. J. K. Rowling was once a TEFL teacher in Portugal!'

TRAINING ROUTES

Initial teacher training comes in many shapes and sizes. As the diagram shows, the first thing to do is decide which of the four main options relate to your circumstances. Once you've clarified this you can look at what training routes are available.

UNDERGRADUATE OPTIONS
An undergraduate can decide to take one of three main routes: a BEd (Bachelor of Education), a BA (Bachelor of Arts) with QTS, or a BSc (Bachelor of Science) with QTS.

POSTGRADUATE OPTIONS
As a postgraduate you'll already have done a degree in a specific subject. To gain QTS you'll need to choose which route best suits your situation. Some courses are taken at universities or colleges, while others can be taken in a school. The most popular of these courses is the PGCE (Postgraduate Certificate of Education). There is also the SCITT (School Centred Initial Teacher Training) and the Teach First Programme.

POSTGRADUATE EMPLOYMENT-BASED OPTIONS
It's now possible to be employed by a school while you train to become a teacher. There are three main options to choose from if

you decide this is the route for you. They are the GTP (Graduate Teacher Programme), the RTP (Registered Teacher Programme) and the OTTP (Overseas Trained Teacher Programme).

KATE BUCKLEY, GRADUATE TEACHER PROGRAMME TRAINEE

What is your role in education?

'I am on the GTP course with Indirect through Hull University. I am a graduate trainee in a substantive post which means I get paid as an unqualified teacher as I train. I teach key stage 4 Drama and AS/A2 level.'

When did you first become interested in teaching?

'I finished my degree at St Martin's and got a job in a school as a teaching assistant and technician. When I watched other teachers at work I thought, "I could do this!" The school management team recommended the GTP course, which they were already involved in, and I went from there.'

What qualifications/training do you have?

'I have a second class honours degree in drama and a BTEC National diploma in performing arts. I have 10 GCSEs and one A level in Art. I also have Equity status, which means I am recognised as a professional actress.'

What is a typical day like?

'I arrive in school at 8.15am for the morning meeting. I register my year 9 form and read any notices and follow up any issues to do with individual tutees. There are two lessons before break. I also teach art, and some of these lessons are in the morning. After the lessons have finished I tend to spend break cleaning up the art rooms and putting the equipment away. If I have a free lesson before lunch then I spend it working on my reflective journal for the course or collecting evidence for my assignments. I could also be required to ring parents if there is an issue with a certain student or perhaps I'll plan for lessons later in the week and do odd jobs like booking space for practical lessons to be taught. Lunchtime lasts for an hour and I always try to give myself 30 minutes to sit in the staffroom and eat my lunch and chat to friends and colleagues. The rest of the lunch hour is spent planning, marking, having meetings etc. I teach a further two lessons after lunch and then spend about 15 minutes clearing away equipment or tidying the workspace. At 3.30pm I usually have an hour-long meeting for various things like departmental issues, full staff meetings or meetings with parents. I then check my emails and do anything urgent for the next day and try to leave school between 5 and 5.30pm.'

How many hours do you work in an average week?
'It can change from week to week depending on how busy I am but usually between 38 and 42 hours.'

What advice would you give to somebody pursuing a career in this field?
'If you fancy the GTP course then make sure you read up on all the aspects of course requirements. You need to be very, very organised and be able to pre-plan everything you do. You also need a lot of confidence.'

What could a job like yours lead to?
'You could teach in a mainstream school or a drama school. You could go in to a career in acting.'

THE QTS ASSESSMENT-ONLY OPTION

This option is available to people who have already been working in schools in various roles, for example as an instructor in an independent school. You can gain QTS status enabling you to become a professional teacher.

THE GRADUATE TEACHER TRAINING REGISTRY (GTTR)

To apply for any Postgraduate Certificate in Education courses you will need to complete an application online through the Graduate Teacher Training Registry (GTTR). The application fee is currently £12 and you cannot submit more than one application in the same cycle. You should also consult the relevant prospectuses to research courses and to check you can satisfy the admission requirements. See www.gttr.ac.uk for more details.

The following tables chart these training routes in more detail to help you decide the best option for you.

UNDERGRADUATE OPTIONS

	What are the entry requirements?	How long does the course last?	Where can you do the course?	What is the course content?	Who would this type of course suit?	What appeal does the course have?	Other details
BEd	They can vary depending on the institution but usually a minimum of five GCSEs (grades A–C) including English and Maths and two A levels or equivalent qualification, at least one of which must be in a National Curriculum subject.*	Usually three or four years full time or four to six years part time.	At many universities or colleges of further education. There are well over 50 undergraduate training providers around the country (see page 98).	This can vary. The four-year course includes 32 weeks in the classroom with emphasis on a specialist subject. The three-year course includes 24 weeks in the classroom and is a general primary teaching degree.	Most suited to primary teaching and usually taken by younger students either straight from school or after a gap year.	It offers an honours degree in education. It's very structured and you are under close supervision of a college tutor. It introduces you slowly into teaching and there's plenty of chance to observe before you teach.	There are a few variations to the BEd course. A shortened two-year course is available for priority secondary subjects. UCAS lists these on its website (www.ucas.com). Applications for a BEd course should be made via UCAS.

	What are the entry requirements?	How long does the course last?	Where can you do the course?	What is the course content?	Who would this type of course suit?	What appeal does the course have?	Other details
BA with QTS	They can vary depending on the institution but usually a minimum of five GCSEs (grades A–C) including English and Maths and two A levels or their equivalent, at least one of which must be in a National Curriculum subject.*	Usually three or four years full time or four to six years part time.	At many universities or colleges of further education. There are well over 50 undergraduate training providers around the country (see page 98).	This is a degree course combined with ITT. It has more emphasis on a specialist subject within the arts. There's some work in schools early on in the course but most of the 24–32 weeks' teaching practice is done in the final two years.	Suited to people with a particular passion for a certain subject. Primary teachers may go on to be a co-ordinator for that subject for the whole school, while secondary teachers will apply for jobs in their specialised subject.	There are two parts to the course. You receive an honours degree in a certain subject in addition to gaining QTS. Once on the course, if you decide teaching isn't for you it's possible to opt out of the QTS and continue with your BA degree.	Decide on your degree subject first and then find an institution that offers the combination with QTS. UCAS lists these on its website (www.ucas.com) Applications for a BA with QTS course should be made via UCAS.

	What are the entry requirements?	How long does the course last?	Where can you do the course?	What is the course content?	Who would this type of course suit?	What appeal does the course have?	Other details
BSc with QTS	They can vary depending on the institution but usually a minimum of five GCSEs (grades A–C) including English and Maths and two A levels or equivalent qualification, at least one of which must be in a National Curriculum subject.*	Usually three or four years full time or four to six years part time.	At many universities or colleges of further education. There are well over 50 undergraduate training providers around the country (see page 98).	This is a degree course combined with ITT. It has more emphasis on a specialist subject within the sciences. There's some work in schools early on in the course but most of the 24–32 weeks' teaching practice is done in the final two years.	Suited to people with a particular passion for a certain subject. Primary teachers may go on to be a co-ordinator for that subject for the whole school, while secondary teachers will apply for jobs in their specialised subject.	There are two parts to the course. You receive an honours degree in a certain subject in addition to gaining QTS. Once on the course, if you decide teaching isn't for you it's possible to opt out of the QTS and continue with your BSc degree.	Decide on your degree subject first and then find an institution that offers the combination with QTS. UCAS lists these on its website (www.ucas.com). Applications for a BSc with QTS course should be made via UCAS.

* If you were born after 1 September 1979 you must have a grade C in a science subject at GCSE level to teach up to key stage 3.

POSTGRADUATE OPTIONS

	What are the entry requirements?	How long does the course last?	Where can you do the course?	What is the course content?	Who would this type of course suit?	What appeal does the course have?	Other details
PGCE	A UK undergraduate degree or equivalent. For secondary teaching the degree should relate to the subject you're going to teach. If you're doing a primary PGCE your degree should be in a subject relevant to the National Curriculum.*	One year full time. A few institutions offer a two-year part-time course for people with other responsibilities such as a family.	There are well over 100 courses for postgraduates wanting to go into teaching. You can find out which institutions offer the PGCE course on the UCAS website www.ucas.com (see also page 98).	The content varies slightly according to where you study. Most courses are organised in blocks, so you are either attending lectures or out on teaching practice. You'll need to do various assignments related to your subject and teaching in general.	Usually taken by people who want to go into secondary teaching and who have graduated in the last couple of years, but some primary courses are available. This type of course would suit people who are very organised and can work well under pressure.	The government may pay your fees for the course and you may also be eligible for a tax-free bursary of £6,000. A PGCE also enables you to make a smoother transition from university to work as you are still being taught in lectures.	You will also need five GCSEs (grades A–C) including English and Maths.* Applications should be made through the Graduate Teaching Training Registry. More information available on their website: www.gttr.ac.uk

	What are the entry requirements?	How long does the course last?	Where can you do the course?	What is the course content?	Who would this type of course suit?	What appeal does the course have?	Other details
SCITT	A UK undergraduate degree or equivalent is needed. For secondary teaching the degree should relate to the subject you're going to teach. If you're doing primary SCITT your degree should be in a subject relevant to the National Curriculum.*	Usually one year full time.	Nearly all the training is done in a base school. Some placements may be arranged at other schools to provide contrasting experiences. Many individual schools offer the course. Look on the TTA website to see who offers the schemes: www.canteach. gov.uk.	The course emphasises classroom management and competence and 'full' teaching will only be done after many observations and part-lesson teaching. You're assigned an experienced teacher from the school as a mentor.	It would suit graduates wanting to teach in primary, middle, secondary, sixth-form or specialist colleges. It would also suit those who want to do nearly all their training in a classroom.	You're working very closely with one school. The course is taught by practising teachers and is often tailored towards local teaching needs. There are plenty of lesson observations in the initial stages.	SCITT courses are very practical but also involve a lot of theory and study work. You will need to keep very detailed logs and complete essays to a high standard. Applications should be made through the Graduate Teaching Training Registry website: www.gttr.ac.uk

	What are the entry requirements	How long does the course last?	Where can you do the course?	What is the course content?	Who would this type of course suit?	What appeal does the course have?	Other details
Teach First	You must have a minimum of 300 UCAS tariff points (equivalent to 3 Bs at A level) and a 2:1 or above at degree level. At least 40% of your degree needs to have been in a relevant National Curriculum subject.*	A two-year course working in challenging secondary schools.	The course is currently available only in Greater London and Greater Manchester.	It's largely up to the individual school with guidance from the Teach First organisation. The Teaching Standards must be covered. The course involves planned observation and gradual teaching under the supervision of your mentor.	It would suit top graduates who show competence in leadership skills, creativity, initiative, teamwork and communication. aims to build the educational leaders	You can qualify as a teacher and do leadership training at the same time. It enables you to gain experience of the management side of teaching and have been initially of the future.	It is run by an independent organisation aimed at targeting high-flying graduates who may not thinking about a career in teaching.

* You will have to have a C or equivalent in GCSE Maths and English Language. If you were born after 1 September 1979 you must have a grade C in a science subject at GCSE level to teach up to key stage 3.

	POSTGRADUATE EMPLOYMENT-BASED OPTIONS						
	What are the entry requirements?	How long does the course last?	Where can you do the course?	What is the course content?	Who would this type of course suit?	What appeal does the course have?	Other details
GTP	A bachelor's degree and a C or equivalent in GCSE Maths and English Language.*	One year full time. If you have substantial teaching experience you may be able to train in a shorter time. The minimum training time is three months.	In an English or Welsh maintained school as long as they employ you as an unqualified teacher. Visit the TTA website to find out more: www.canteach.gov.uk.	It is very practical and, depending on the school, you may feel like you've been thrown in at the deep end. There's often some teaching from the word go and an awful lot of paperwork, including essays, log books and skills tests.	It's good for mature students because you can earn as you train (an unqualified teacher currently earns between £13,938 and £22,041 in England and Wales). It would suit well organised people who want to get into the classroom as soon as possible.	You work as a teacher in one school (with a short second placement). There's a lot of independent study and only a few course meetings. You are affiliated to a university so your qualification will come from them.	Designated recommending bodies (DRBs) deliver the GTP. Apply to your local DRB for a GTP place or apply direct to the GTP provider. The TTA has information about these routes.

	What are the entry requirements?	How long does the course last?	Where can you do the course?	What is the course content?	Who would this type of course suit?	What appeal does the course have?	Other details
RTP	You must have completed two years of higher education, e.g. two years of a degree course, HND or DipHE (the equivalent of 240 CATS points). Ideally you should already be working at a school as an unqualified teacher.*	Because the course allows non-graduates with some experience of higher education to complete their degree while qualifying to teach at the same time, it is usually a two-year course. It may be shorter if you already have considerable teaching experience.	You can complete the course in an English or Welsh maintained school, which works with a higher education institution, as long as they employ you as an unqualified teacher. Visit the TTA website to find out more: www.canteach.gov.uk.	The course is both work-based and includes academic study. It is often tailored to the individual needs of the trainee and is designed to extend your subject knowledge while you gain QTS. As with the GTP there is a lot of paperwork.	It tends to suit mature students who do not have a degree. You can earn as you train (an unqualified teacher currently earns between £13,938 and £22,041 in England and Wales). It would suit well organised people.	It allows people who do not have a degree to go into teaching. It often attracts mature people who are wanting a career change. You can complete a degree at the same time as gaining QTS.	You need to make sure that your experience in higher education is in a relevant subject. It's an intense course as you're also completing your degree. Make sure you can afford to train for a full two years.

	What are the entry requirements?	How long does the course last?	Where can you do the course?	What is the course content?	Who would this type of course suit?	What appeal does the course have?	Other details
OTTP	You will need the equivalent of a UK bachelor's degree and have trained as a teacher in the EU.* Contact the National Academic Recognition Centre at www.naric.org.uk to find out if your qualifications are recognised and acceptable in this country.	The training is tailored to the individual so the length of the course depends on the extent of additional training needed. However, the maximum amount of time you can spend on the OTTP is one year. The course can start and finish at any point in the year.	You will be assessed while employed by a school, so the course will take place in the school you're working in.	You're assessed against the QTS standards and have a final assessment similar to the GTP course.	It suits anyone who has trained as a teacher in the EU and now wants to work in England or Wales. If you have qualified overseas you can work without QTS for up to four years but completing the OTTP enables you to teach permanently in the UK.	It enables people who qualified as a teacher in a different country to work at the same rate of pay as teachers who qualified in this country.	If you qualified in a European Economic Area country or Switzerland you may be eligible for QTS without further assessment. Contact gtce.org.uk to have your qualifications assessed. The Teaching Development Agency may cover your costs up to £1,250 as well as the final assessment costs.

* You will need a C or equivalent in GCSE Maths and English Language. If you were born after 1 September 1979 you must have a grade C in a science subject at GCSE level to teach up to key stage 3.

QTS ASSESSMENT-ONLY OPTION

	What are the entry requirements?	How long does the course last?	Where can you do the course?	What is the course content?	Who would this type of course suit?	What appeal does the course have?	Other details
QTS	You must already be working as an unqualified teacher at an independent school or maybe as an instructor of some kind. You must also have a degree and a C or equivalent in GCSE Maths and English Language. If you were born after 1 September 1979 you must have a C in a science subject at GCSE to teach up to key stage 3.	It can take up to a year to complete but can start and finish at any time during the year. You need to compile and submit a portfolio of evidence to show that you have met all the QTS standards and are a competent classroom teacher. There will be a day-long assessment visit at the school you're working in.	The course is done in your own time through the compilation of evidence for the QTS standards. The University of Gloucestershire administers this process for England. It is not yet available in Wales.	It is purely compiling evidence over the year on how you have met the standards. The University of Gloucestershire will provide all the information on these standards. You'll need to arrange an appropriate time for the assessment visit.	Anyone already teaching as an unqualified teacher in England at an independent school or as an instructor (e.g. at a field centre). If you want to continue teaching, but in an institution other than an independent school, this is a way to gain QTS.	It's very much independent study and requires only one full day of assessment. You can stay employed at the school you're in whilst gathering evidence for you portfolio. Your fees will normally be covered by the TTA.	You must contact the University of Gloucestershire directly if you want to apply for this. Tel. 01242 532895; email: gtsassessmentonly@glos.ac.uk.

SOME FINANCIAL INCENTIVES

The government is committed to getting more people into teaching, and there are many financial incentives which are worth considering:

- People embarking on a PGCE may be able to have their fees paid in full by the government.

- Graduates intending to train as secondary teachers in priority subject specialisms may be eligible for a tax-free bursary of £9,000 as from September 2006, plus a 'golden hello' of £2,500–5,000 if they successfully complete their induction period. The priority subjects are Applied ICT, Applied Science, Dance, Design Technology, Drama, Engineering, English, ICT, Manufacturing, Mathematics, Modern Languages, Music, Religious Education and Science.

- Graduates in secondary non-priority subjects and all primary trainees will continue receiving a £6,000 tax-free bursary. The non-priority subjects are Applied Art and Design, Applied Business, Art and Design, Business Studies, Citizenship, Classics, Geography, Health and Social Care, History, Leisure and Tourism, Media Studies, Physical Education and Social Sciences.

CHAPTER 4

Is teaching for me?

Teaching can be a very rewarding profession. But do you have the attributes to enable you to become a successful teacher? You don't just have to like children and enjoy their company. Teaching is also about enabling children to learn, not just about a particular subject, but about life skills and how to become responsible adults. As a teacher you have a fundamental role not only in helping children achieve their goals academically, but also in helping them to develop socially.

'I will never forget the look on my students' faces when they realised they had won a national award for their environmental project – the thrill of having their work recognised at the highest level still lives with them to this day.'

Jarvis Hayes, head of department, Settle

Primary school teachers are well known for their ability to create the right emotional climate for learning and they're usually expert communicators who have a sixth sense for what children need to move them forward. In primary school there's also the need to feel comfortable talking with children about their feelings, as well as an ability to understand children's moods!

JOANNE WATFORD, PRIMARY SCHOOL TEACHER
What is your role in education?
'I am a class teacher of a year 5 class (key stage 2)'.

When did you first become interested in teaching?
'I think I've always wanted to be a teacher. I love being with children and like organising things.'

What qualifications/training do you have?
'I did a four-year BA with QTS in geography and gained an upper second class degree.'

What is a typical day like?
'I arrive at school at 8.30am and do any photocopying or preparation in the classroom for the day. At 9am I register my class and give out any important information and then I start on the first lesson. We have an hour and a half before playtime and this is usually filled with work for the literacy hour incorporating other cross-curricular topics such as reading about the history of our local town. At break I go to the staff room for ten minutes before going back to the classroom to prepare anything that needs getting out for the next session. Between playtime and lunchtime I often teach a more practical lesson like music, art or PE. I have an hour for lunch. I take my class down to the canteen and check that they are all OK, then I go to the staffroom for my lunch. At 1pm I often run a sports club like netball or football. After lunch it's straight back to the classroom to wait for my class to arrive. We have one session before afternoon playtime, which is usually spent doing maths, and then after playtime I teach another subject, often with the same topic as the rest of the day, but deliver it through something like science or design or information technology. At 3.30pm, when the children go home, I either have a staff meeting for an hour or spend time marking work, putting up displays, meeting with parents or planning work for later. I get home at about 5pm. I

---

tend to give myself a few hours' rest before doing about an hour's more school work in the evening.'

What hours do you work in an average week?
'Probably about 40 to 45 hours including the work I do at home.'

What advice would you give somebody interested in pursuing a career in this field?
'Make sure you have a love of young children. In a primary school you could be teaching children anywhere from the ages of 3 to 11, so this is important. Make sure you can manage your time well and don't mind a lot of interaction (or interfering) from parents.'

What are the highs and lows of the job?
'The highs are the children and the enthusiasm they bring to the work you've planned (I think this is very different in secondary schools). The money is OK too and the holidays are much needed. The lows would have to be the amount of marking, paperwork and administration that needs doing and the time that it takes to do it all.'

What could a job like yours lead on to?
'It could lead to a variety of things, really, depending on where your interests lie. You could become in charge of a certain subject for your school, become a deputy head, decide to specialise in special educational needs etc., the list is endless really and depends on personal strengths and preference.'

If you're planning to work in a secondary school you'll be considered a subject specialist. This means that you'll need to have a love of your subject that can be communicated to your students, as well as being really knowledgeable in your subject area (qualified to degree level) and prepared to keep up with the latest developments. Communication skills and empathy are important too, together with meticulous organisation to cope with everything that is thrown at you.

Below is a list of important things a teacher needs to be able to encourage children to learn. Have a look at them and ask yourself, 'Could I teach children to ...

- be confident individuals?

- grow into responsible citizens?

- stay motivated in all they do?

- lead a healthy lifestyle?

- make positive contributions?

- show respect to others?

- enjoy and achieve?'

If you feel you could do all of these, perhaps you need to think about whether or not you also have the following attributes. Are you:

- patient?

- creative?

- organised?

- self-motivated?

- willing to listen?

- willing to learn?

Do you have:

- stamina?

- imagination?

- enthusiasm for your subject?

- a good knowledge of your subject?

- the ability to keep cool under pressure?

- good time management skills?

- a sense of humour?

- determination?

If you answered 'yes' to most of these, you probably are a good candidate for becoming a teacher. Why not have a look at the three charts below? These have been compiled using parts of the Teaching Standards you will have to pass if you want to qualify as a teacher.

Put a tick in one of the boxes alongside each statement to show how you think you rate against each of the qualities needed. Tick 1 if you do not have that skill or attribute at all, 5 if you have it in abundance, or an intermediate score if you fall in between.

Values and practice					
	1	2	3	4	5
I really enjoy working with children or young people					
I have high expectations of people and would be committed to raising the education achievement of students					
I have good organisational skills					
I respect people for their differences					
I can promote positive values and am prepared to be a role model					

	1	2	3	4	5
I would like to contribute to the corporate life of a school					
I like to evaluate what I do in order to improve					
I am interested in my own professional development and am willing to seek advice to help me improve					
I feel I could communicate sensitively with parents and carers					

Knowledge and understanding					
	1	2	3	4	5
I am prepared to reach the required standards for the Qualified Teacher Status skills tests in numeracy, literacy and ICT					
I am aware that people have different learning needs and am prepared to learn more about the special educational needs Code of Practice					
I understand how students' learning can be affected by other life experiences (e.g. social, cultural and emotional background)					
I have a secure knowledge of a particular subject (particularly important for secondary teaching)					

	1	2	3	4	5
I am prepared to learn the National Curriculum for my subject area and wider subjects (e.g. literacy, numeracy, key skills, citizenship and PSHE)					
I am prepared to learn how to manage students' behaviour positively					

'Everyone went swimming, but because of my disability from polio it took me a year to learn. All the other kids learned quickly and I was lagging behind. It was distressing for me because I could see it was down to my disability. Miss Singleton didn't give up on me. She designed a float that I could tie to my leg to keep it buoyant. Once I could stay up I learned to swim within a couple of months. That is one of my fondest memories of school.'

Ade Adepitan, paralympian and TV presenter

Teaching: planning, monitoring, class management					
	1	2	3	4	5
I am prepared to learn lesson planning skills, including how to set appropriate learning objectives and use specific teaching techniques and appropriate equipment					
I understand the need to make learning enjoyable and interesting for all the students I teach, including those from a wide range of cultural and ethnic groups					

	1	2	3	4	5
I am prepared to work with students of all abilities including those with specific barriers to learning (e.g. disabilities or behavioural problems)					
I understand that other professionals such as teaching assistants work alongside teachers and am prepared to work positively with these people					
I am willing to give immediate and constructive feedback					
I am prepared to monitor and assess individuals' progress, including keeping careful records on individual students					
I would be prepared to report sensitively on the progress of students to parents and other professionals					

So how did you do? If the majority of your answers were 4s and 5s then teaching might really be the career for you. You seem to have the basic requirements to be successful in the classroom and the skills to promote learning. However, don't worry too much if you recognise that your specific knowledge or skills need to be developed – this is the purpose of your teaching course.

If your answers were mainly 3s for all three boxes then perhaps you need to stop to think a little bit more about whether teaching really is for you. Perhaps you could do some more research into the qualities required to be a teacher and try to improve on these?

If you scored mainly 1s and 2s, particularly in the first section, teaching is probably the wrong career for you. Why not think again about what your strengths are and look at some other books in this series to see what would suit you better?

'From the age of 12, I took sailing lessons at Cumbrae, an island west of Largs. It was a great joy to be coached by someone who believed in everybody he worked with. He motivated us by making it fun while we learned to sail, and he encouraged us to be competitive, which I definitely gained from.'

Emma Richards, yachtswoman

COULD DO BETTER? SOME QUOTES FROM SCHOOL REPORTS

Dame Judi Dench: 'Judi would be a very good pupil if she lived in this world.'

Stephen Fry: 'He has glaring faults and they have certainly glared at us this term.'

Harry Enfield (at age 6): 'Very talkative. Unfortunately what he has to say is not always relevant.'

Sir Winston Churchill (at primary school): 'Is a constant trouble to everybody and is always in some scrape or other.'

Carol Vorderman (at age 8): 'Carol has a masterly hold over mathematical computation which should prove profitable later on.'

Jeremy Paxman: 'His stubbornness is in his nature, and could be an asset when directed to sound ends. He must learn tact while not losing his outspokenness.'

John Lennon (on his 'leaver' report): 'A fairly responsible adult who might go far.'

Bob Geldof: not available – though he did admit in an interview in *Hello* magazine that he used to create his own school reports in order to appease his father.

Source: *Could Do Better*, edited by Catherine Hurley, published by Simon and Schuster

GETTING SOME PRACTICAL EXPERIENCE

Whatever your score on the above exercise, there's really no substitute for actually experiencing teaching to help you decide if this is a career for you. Try to make contact with a local school who'll welcome you as an observer (perhaps your old school or one you have contacts in), or try to fix up some formal work experience through your school or careers office. It's very revealing to get the chance to talk to a range of teachers about what the job is really like on a day-to-day basis.

One of the longest school days in the world is in Japan, where students work for 6 hours per day in classes of up to 40 students and also have extended homework after school. They have six weeks' holiday in the summer and then two-week breaks between the two other terms in the school year. There is also homework set for every holiday break. Many students also attend Juku (cram schools) to help them pass the rigorous examination system. These take place for 2–3 hours a day after normal schooling and students attend 3–4 days a week. Juku can start in nursery school.

Many schools will allow you to work in small groups (under the supervision of the teacher) as an unpaid classroom assistant, though you may need to be police checked: the rules around working with children are now very stringent (see box). This kind of work will begin to give you an idea what it's like to work with young people in an education setting.

POLICE VETTING PROCEDURE FOR PEOPLE WORKING WITH CHILDREN

The Criminal Records Bureau (CRB) provides criminal record checks for people working with children and young people, reducing the risk that unsuitable people can gain employment with children. The CRB aims to help employers and voluntary organisations make safer recruitment decisions through a service called Disclosure. The Bureau issues three types of Disclosure, each representing a different level of check. Work with children and young people or with vulnerable adults qualifies for the most detailed checks.

A CRB check involves an automatic search of the Police National Computer. This would reveal whether a person had been convicted, cautioned, reprimanded or given a warning for a criminal offence, including those relating to sexual offences/cautions. If the position for which the CRB check is required involves working with children or vulnerable adults, and the relevant boxes on the application form are crossed, the CRB also checks List 99, the POCA (Protection of Children Act) list and POVA (Protection of Vulnerable Adults) list. The check could also be used to reveal any information held by the DfES under Section 142 of the Education Act 2002 on those considered unsuitable or banned from working with children.

Applicants for the post in question are asked to complete a disclosure form giving details of their record, if any, and giving their consent to a search being carried out. This is then forwarded to CRB so that details may be verified and a full search carried out. When the application is processed, the CRB sends out a copy of the Disclosure, containing any information revealed during its searches, to the applicant and to the person who countersigned your form (normally the prospective employer). Prospective employers have a duty to treat this information with sensitivity, store it appropriately and to retain it only for as long as is necessary. Each Disclosure will show the date on which it was printed. Disclosures do not carry a pre-determined period of validity because a conviction or other matter could be recorded against the subject of the Disclosure at any time after it is issued.

FASCINATING FACTS

Statistics from the National Association of Schoolmasters and Union of Women Teachers released in 2005 showed that 2,038 allegations of misconduct had been made against its members since 1991, but that the number of accusations is increasing each year. However, of all incidents recorded, only 81 cases have resulted in a conviction.

SARAH FOSTER, ENTERPRISE CO-ORDINATOR
What is your current role in education?
'I'm Enterprise Co-ordinator at an Education Business Partnership (EBP). EBPs provide the interface between education and business for the mutual benefit of both parties. My role involves organising enterprising projects to support the curriculum in primary and secondary schools. All of the projects involve business volunteers and include initiatives such as design challenges, environmental projects and fundraising schemes. The projects are usually really successful and that's because of the 'real life' dimension. Young people see the relevance of that and it really motivates them.'

When did you first become interested in working in education/with young people?
'I became interested in education whilst at university because I wanted to teach my subject (history). It was something that interested me and so I wanted to get young people interested in history too.'

Why did you decide to work in this particular area?
'I trained as a teacher but decided I wanted to do something else in education. To be honest I fell into this area by accident. I started off working on a mentoring scheme and then this post came up and it looked really interesting so I went for it. I'm really glad that I did.'

What qualifications/training do you have that are relevant to the role?

'I have a teaching qualification and some experience of working in business, both of which are relevant to the role as it's vital that you can appreciate the perspectives and agendas of both educationalists and the business community.'

What particular skills are necessary for this job?

'You have to be pretty well organised as I manage lots of projects simultaneously. The ability to negotiate is important as I'm often trying to ensure that both schools' and businesses' objectives are met. Creativity is also really important as a lot of the ideas for new projects have to be generated by me.'

Describe a typical day

'There really is no such thing as a typical day in this job. A recent day was a trade fair at a local school where students exhibited work relating to all the enterprise projects they had been involved in throughout the school year. The day began at around 8.30am when I arrived at the school. I helped teachers and students to set up the hall (moving furniture etc.), then we spent the rest of the morning helping students to display their work and prepare for the judges. At lunchtime guests started to arrive and the next few hours were spent talking to students, business people and members of the community. At about 2pm I delivered a speech about the project and was then interviewed by a local radio station and newspaper. Once all the guests had gone, the hall had to be put back and this involved removing all the stands and generally tidying up. We finished at about 4.30. As you can see, all very hectic and varied!'

What are the working conditions like in your job?

'Working conditions are good. I work a regular nine-to-five day but it is so varied and I am out and about so much visiting schools and businesses that time just flies by. Holidays are 22 days plus 13 statutory days (based on the local council entitlement), so a total of 35 days a year.'

What are the highs and lows of the job?
'Seeing projects come together is the highlight of the job but sometimes things do go wrong, which can be hard to deal with when you've spent months of hard work setting a project up. Thankfully that doesn't happen often.'

What advice would you give somebody who is interested in pursuing a career in this field?
'This type of role is a great stepping stone to other things and opens so many doors for opportunities in education. My advice would be to ignore the salary (which might not be fantastic compared to, say, teaching; around £20,000) as it will help you to develop so much.'

What could a job like this lead on to?
'This type of job can lead on to so many other areas of project work in education – working for a trust or charity or a Local Education Authority, for example. The job is so varied that you develop lots of transferable skills.'

CHAPTER 5

What should I do next?

The previous chapters of this book have highlighted the range of different roles that are possible within teaching. The interviews have also outlined the highs and lows of working in teaching, together with the skills and qualifications required of teachers. You should now have a pretty good idea of whether a career in teaching is something you're serious about pursuing – so what next?

'All Bill Bowen had to do was lower his beautiful, melodious voice, bring about a slight shift in timbre, and the children's hair would stand on end. In assembly, he would persuade 120 children to sit still and listen to classical music. He was always extremely theatrical and did things no other teacher would do. When he took us for hymn practice every week, he used to thrust and stab with his baton at the "foul fiends and hobgoblins" in "To Be a Pilgrim".'

Jonathan Stroud, children's author

This chapter explains the steps you need to take in order to get into teaching.

Step 1: Decide which age range you'd like to teach

This is very much a personal preference. The interviews in the book will help you to find out about the highs and lows of working with children of different ages, but it's likely that you'll already have a gut reaction as to which school phase you feel most attracted to. Remember that your decision is never final: it's possible to do conversation courses or further training that prepare you for working with another age range. Make sure you get some proper experience of teaching in the different age ranges. Some people think working with young children will be lovely, but then realise how demanding they are in the classroom; others think that teaching their specialist subject in a secondary school is the best route, but soon discover that many students do not share the teacher's passion for their subject! It pays to think carefully at this stage.

Step 2: Choose your training route

As we discussed in Chapter 3, there are now a number of routes into teaching, depending on your previous qualifications or the type of training you'd like to follow. The first step is to decide which of these routes is most appropriate. Study the tables in Chapter 3 carefully, and consider the options open to you. You might also find it useful to discuss your options with a careers officer, a teacher or another adult.

Step 3: Decide where you'd like to train

This very much depends on your personal circumstances. If you're already settled in one part of the country, it's likely that you'll choose to train close to home. Alternatively, you may fancy a change of scene and move to a new area to undertake your training, either at a university or a school. There's a detailed listing of universities and colleges offering teacher training courses in Chapter 6.

Step 4: Find out more about potential training venues

There's no substitute for detailed information about the possible training venues available to you. It's likely that there'll be a choice, so make sure you send off for information packs, visit the university/college or school you're interested in and try to talk to other people who have trained there. Public information is available about the 'star ratings' of many university departments for the quality of their teaching and research, so do ask about this when you visit. You might also want to find out about the following:

● how the training is structured

● the kind of support offered to trainee teachers

● what you can expect from the schools you'll work in

● the success of previous trainees in finding a job

● what they see as the strengths (and if they're honest, weaknesses) of the university/college or school

● how flexible the training is.

You may also wish to compile a list of the questions that are most important to you, which will depend on your circumstances.

Step 5: Complete your application

Whatever route you choose, there'll be a formal application process to follow, usually involving an application form and an interview. As with any application procedure, you should take this seriously, as you'll probably be competing with other people for places. Be upbeat about yourself, stressing all the positive things you've done, but **never** exaggerate or lie on your application form. It's always a good idea to get someone else to read over your completed application form before sending it off – they might spot mistakes you miss and can often help you to phrase things more professionally.

Step 6: Attend the interview

Hopefully, you'll be invited to an informal interview to discuss your suitability for the course you chose. This is your opportunity to impress the training provider and find out more about what they have to offer. Don't be afraid to ask difficult questions, as you need to be sure that this is the right course – and most appropriate training venue – for you. Other, more general, advice on interviews is contained in a range of other Trotman books (see Chapter 6).

Step 7: Make your mind up

If your interview goes well you'll shortly be offered a place on your chosen course – now it's decision time for you! If you've attended interviews at more than one training provider, you'll need to weigh up the pros and cons of each. Remember that whatever you decide you'll be signing up for at least a year of your life, so it pays to make a careful decision.

> FASCINATING FACTS
>
> **The author Phillip Pullman, the rock star Sting and the Olympic medallist Brendan Foster were all teachers. The rock guitarist Brian May, who made his name as part of the hit band Queen, taught maths for a while before his music career took off.**

DURING YOUR TRAINING

There are now very strict criteria which you'll need to meet in order to gain Qualified Teacher Status (QTS). During your training the most significant element is your teaching practice, where you get the chance to learn the ropes of teaching. This is when you have the chance to demonstrate the quality standards expected of teachers by the government. Great teachers make teaching look easy, but remember that teaching is a complex and highly skilled activity, and you're bound to make lots of mistakes to begin with. Be patient – and keep in mind that you'll never be the finished article when it comes to teaching. Teachers carry on learning throughout their careers.

It's vital during your training to learn as much as you can about the psychology of learning. This underpins everything you're trying to do as a teacher, and it helps to remind yourself that, just as doctors are experts in healing, so teachers should be experts in learning.

'He put me in the school football team. I was a couple of years too young, but he put me in with all the older boys. He just understood me and my needs and he didn't judge me.'

Vinnie Jones, actor and ex-footballer

The most important person during your training course is your teacher mentor – the person whose role it is to support you as you acquire the knowledge and skills of a teacher. If this person is not doing their job properly, then you're likely to find things really heavy going, so don't be afraid to lean on your teacher mentor for their advice and support.

Unless you qualify in Wales, you will be required to sit the Qualified Teacher Skills tests in literacy, ICT and numeracy to ensure you have the necessary level of expertise. The bottom line is that if you can't reach the desired standard you won't be able to teach.

FINDING YOUR FIRST JOB

When you qualify as a teacher you'll receive a certificate from the government which is your licence to teach. At this stage you're given the rather obvious title of 'newly qualified teacher' or NQT, a term which is recognised throughout the profession. Your next task is to land your first job.

> **The compulsory age for starting school varies considerably across Europe. In England it is five, in Belgium it is six and in Denmark it is seven or eight, depending on your date of birth.**

If you've decided that classroom teaching is for you – whether in a nursery, primary or secondary school – the *Times Educational*

Supplement (or the *TES*, as most teachers know it), which is published every Friday, will be your main source of reference. It's crammed full of hundreds of teaching vacancies, and represents the most comprehensive listing available in the UK. Posts that are specially suited to NQTs are indicated as such, and there are separate sections for the different phases of education. Other useful sources of information on jobs include the union and subject magazines, and if you're training through a university, the internal information boards there, which schools find useful when recruiting NQTs.

It's worth noting that in some subjects or age ranges teachers are in short supply, but in others it can actually be quite hard to find work, especially if you restrict yourself geographically (see box).

PRIORITY SUBJECT AREAS
The new priority subject list in schools effective from September 2006 (and attracting additional bursaries and golden hellos – see page 73) includes the following:

- Applied ICT
- Applied Science
- Design Technology
- Drama
- Dance
- Engineering
- English

- ICT
- Manufacturing
- Mathematics
- Modern Languages
- Music
- Religious Education
- Science

If you're planning to teach in the further education sector, a separate list of 'shortage subjects' applies – check out www.teachernet.gov.uk.

> **FASCINATING FACTS**
>
> **The earliest you can leave school in England is 16; in Belgium you can leave at 15 but you have to continue in part-time education until you're 18; and in Denmark you must receive at least nine years of education, which means that most students leave sometime around their seventeenth birthday.**

Some NQTs are lucky enough to be offered a job in the school where they trained. This is most common for people who have taken a course with a very strong element of school-based training. The advantage of this, apart from not having to go through the hassle of the application process, is that you already know many of the staff and students at this school. You also know what the school is **really** like, and how well you fit in.

You may, however, decide that you'd like to work in education but not as a classroom teacher. Several of the interviews and profiles in this book come from people who have chosen to work in a teaching-style role outside schools, that supplements the work done there. Vacancies in these areas are also sometimes advertised in the *TES*. It's also worth scanning through the education specials of the other broadsheet newspapers for job adverts, and visiting the websites of the organisations you'd like to work for.

Remember that for most of the more senior support roles in education mentioned in this book, you'll need to have Qualified Teacher Status and several years of classroom and school management experience. These options should only be considered once you've established your credentials in the classroom.

Further guidance on the process of applying for jobs and interviews is contained in these Trotman books.

- *Winning CVs for First-Time Job Hunters*, 2nd edn, Kathleen Houston (Trotman, 2004)

- *Winning Interviews for First-Time Job Hunters*, Kathleen Houston (Trotman, 2005)

- *Winning Job-Hunting Strategies for First-Time Job Hunters*, Gary Woodward (Trotman, 2004).

To teach in maintained schools, non-maintained special schools and pupil referral units, you need to register with the General Teaching Council for the country of your choice (see web addresses on page 102). You need to register **before** you begin your first teaching post, including any supply teaching work you undertake. GTCs also deal with serious disciplinary matters concerning the conduct of teachers, with the ultimate sanction of being 'struck off' the register of teachers, which means you'll be unable to teach until you are re-instated.

FAST TRACK TEACHING

If you're a higher flier and are really up for a challenge, you might want to consider the 'Fast Track Teaching' route, which is really a way of fast tracking you into school management (see box). But be warned, entry requirements are very strict and you'll need to be prepared to move around a lot and work in some very challenging schools. For more details visit www.fasttrackteaching.gov.uk.

LIFE IN THE FAST LANE

Liz Robinson's appointment as headteacher of Surrey Square Primary School in 2005 marked a huge milestone for the Fast Track Teaching Programme – she was the first headteacher to be promoted to the top job since the scheme began in 2000.

The programme was introduced as a way of modernising the teaching profession by providing an 'accelerated leadership development programme' to enable talented teachers to progress towards the top leadership roles in schools. Liz enrolled in the first intake of qualified teachers in 2002 and went on to become an assistant head at Charles Dickens Primary School in September 2003 and then deputy head in March 2005.

The Fast Track scheme provides support, training and opportunities for teachers like Liz Robinson, who have shown they have the skills it takes to lead a school to progress to the top. It encourages exceptional teachers to progress at a rate that suits their ability, not their age. Responding to comments about her promotion Liz Robinson pointed out that she had wanted to be a head since becoming a teacher and that the individual support offered by the Fast Track Programme had allowed her to realise her potential as early as possible.

In radio interviews after her appointment she quoted the results of a survey carried out on behalf of the Fast Track programme which showed that 98% of people believe that ability is more important than age when it comes to leadership. However, at the same time, only 4% believe that you should become a headteacher before the age of 30. She explained how this kind of attitude can make it difficult for talented young teachers to feel able to move into leadership roles and how this is at odds with other industries and professions where the best are allowed to rise to the top on the basis of their skills without being judged on their age.

She said: 'I firmly believe if you're good enough you're old enough. If you have the required skills and are able to lead and manage others, your age should definitely not stand in the way of progress. The Fast Track Teaching programme helps teachers who have leadership ambitions to hone their skills and develop as quickly as their ability allows.'

ALTERNATIVE JOBS WORKING WITH YOUNG PEOPLE

If you like the idea of working with young people but the training or jobs described in *Teaching Uncovered* don't really appeal to you, there are plenty of other related roles you can consider.

- Other classroom roles in schools – teaching assistant, learning support assistant, learning mentor (see interview on page 9).

- Other non-teaching roles in schools – including administrator, careers officer, bursar and librarian (see page 31).

- Teaching roles not based in schools – prison or hospital educator, private tuition, further education lecturer, assessor/instructor for work-based training, sports instructor, field studies lecturer.

- Other education-related roles supporting schools – enterprise co-ordinator (see page 85), education psychologist, widening participation officer in a university, wildlife educator, education officer in a museum and many others.

If it's teaching that you're keen on but want to work with adults, then are plenty of openings as an adult education tutor. Enquire at your local FE college for more information.

FINALLY …

As the interviews in this book show, teaching can be a very rewarding career. Indeed, teachers often talk about their level of job satisfaction in a way that few other professions can match – despite the fact that they're often quoted in the press on the pressures of teaching. Seeing children and young people flourish through your efforts is an amazing experience, and contact with youngsters also helps to keep you creative.

If you're prepared to face up to the challenges that teaching can throw at you, not least managing students' behaviour and withstanding the intensity of face-to-face interactions every day, then this may well be the job for you.

On his retirement day, a teacher with thirty years' experience was asked, 'Why did you come into teaching?'

'Because I wanted to change the world,' he replied.

'And did you succeed?' asked his colleague.

'Not really,' he said, sounding a little downbeat. But then his eyes lit up: 'But I think in a small way I changed a thousand worlds.'

CHAPTER 6

Further information

PLACES TO STUDY

These are all the universities and colleges in England and Wales that offer teacher training courses for undergraduates, postgraduates or both.

University of Wales, Aberystwyth	www.aber.ac.uk
Anglia Ruskin University	www.anglia.ac.uk
University of Wales, Bangor	www.bangor.ac.uk
University of Bath	www.bath.ac.uk
Bath Spa University	www.bathspa.ac.uk
University of Birmingham	www.bham.ac.uk
Bishop Grosseteste College	www.bgc.ac.uk
Bradford College	www.bilk.ac.uk
University of Brighton	www.brighton.ac.uk
University of Bristol	www.bris.ac.uk
Brunel University	www.brunel.ac.uk
University of Cambridge	www.cam.ac.uk
Canterbury Christ Church University	www.canterbury.ac.uk
University of Wales Institute, Cardiff	www.uwic.ac.uk
University of Central England	www.uce.ac.uk

Central School of Speech and Drama	www.cssd.ac.uk
University of Chester	www.chester.ac.uk
University of Chichester	www.chiuni.ac.uk
College of St Mark and St John	www.marjon.ac.uk
De Montfort University	www.dmu.ac.uk
University of Derby	www.derby.ac.uk
University of Durham	www.dur.ac.uk
University of East Anglia	www.uea.ac.uk
Edge Hill University	www.edgehill.ac.uk
University of East London	www.uel.ac.uk
University of Exeter	www.exeter.ac.uk
University of Gloucestershire	www.glos.ac.uk
Goldsmiths College	www.goldsmiths.ac.uk
University of Greenwich	www.gre.ac.uk
University of Hertfordshire	www.herts.ac.uk
University of Huddersfield	www.hud.ac.uk
University of Hull	www.hull.ac.uk
Keele University	www.keele.ac.uk
King's College London	www.kcl.ac.uk
Kingston University	www.kingston.ac.uk
University of Leeds	www.leeds.ac.uk
Leeds Metropolitan University	www.lmu.ac.uk
University of Leicester	www.le.ac.uk
Liverpool Hope University	www.hope.ac.uk
Liverpool John Moores University	www.ljmu.ac.uk
London Metropolitan University	www.londonmet.ac.uk
London South Bank University	www.lsbu.ac.uk
Institute of Education, London	www.ioe.ac.uk
Loughborough University	www.lboro.ac.uk
University of Manchester	www.manchester.ac.uk
Manchester Metropolitan University	www.mmu.ac.uk
Middlesex University	www.mdx.ac.uk
Newcastle University	www.ncl.ac.uk
Newham College	www.newham.ac.uk
University of Wales College, Newport	www.newport.ac.uk
North East Wales Institute	www.newi.ac.uk
University of Northampton	www.northampton.ac.uk
Northumbria University	www.northumbria.ac.uk
University of Nottingham	www.nottingham.ac.uk
Nottingham Trent University	www.ntu.ac.uk
Open University	www.open.ac.uk

University of Oxford	www.ox.ac.uk
Oxford Brookes University	www.brookes.ac.uk
University of Plymouth	www.plymouth.ac.uk
University of Portsmouth	www.port.ac.uk
University of Reading	www.rdg.ac.uk
Roehampton University	www.roehampton.ac.uk
Royal Academy of Dance	www.rad.org.uk
University of Sheffield	www.shef.ac.uk
Sheffield Hallam University	www.shu.ac.uk
University of Southampton	www.soton.ac.uk
St Martin's College	www.ucsm.ac.uk
St Mary's College	www.smuc.ac.uk
Staffordshire University	www.staffs.ac.uk
University of Sunderland	www.sunderland.ac.uk
University of Sussex	www.sussex.ac.uk
University of Wales Swansea	www.swan.ac.uk
Swansea Institute of Higher Education	www.sihe.ac.uk
University of Teesside	www.tees.ac.uk
Trinity and All Saints College	www.tasc.ac.uk
Trinity College Carmarthen	www.trinity-cm.ac.uk
University of Warwick	www.warwick.ac.uk
University of the West of England	www.uwe.ac.uk
University of Winchester	www.winchester.ac.uk
University of Wolverhampton	www.wlv.ac.uk
University of Worcester	www.worcester.ac.uk
University of York	www.york.ac.uk
York St John College	www.yorksj.ac.uk

USEFUL AGENCIES

Department for Education and Skills (DfES)
The Department for Education and Skills develops and implements education policies and provides up-to-date information on all aspects of education and training.
www.dfes.gov.uk

Department of Education Northern Ireland
Provides up-to-date information on all aspects of education and training. They develop and implement the policies behind education.
www.deni.gov.uk

Graduate Teacher Training Registry (GTTR)
This is the central organisation that processes applications for postgraduates. Visit their website to find postgraduate ITT courses and vacancies. You can find out more about the application process and apply online.
www.gttr.ac.uk

Independent Schools Council
Provides details about teaching in independent schools.
www.isc.co.uk

National Association for Special Educational Needs
Their website contains information about how to specialise in this area of teaching.
www.nasen.org.uk

Scottish Executive Education Department (SEED)
Responsible for administering policies for the teaching profession in Scotland and provides information on teacher training.
www.teachinginscotland.com

Skill
Skill is the National Bureau for students with disabilities and can give useful information on relevant courses and institutions.
www.skill.org.uk

Teacher Training Agency
In charge of raising standards in schools and attracting the right people into the profession. They can tell you all you need to know about getting into teaching in England and Wales.
www.canteach.gov.uk

Training and Development Agency (TDA)
Provides detailed information about all routes into teaching.
www.tda.gov.uk

Universities and Colleges Admissions Service (UCAS)
For undergraduate ITT courses and to learn more about the application process visit the UCAS website.
www.ucas.com

THE GENERAL TEACHING COUNCILS

These organisations regulate the teaching profession and aim to raise the status of teaching and learning.

Council for England	www.gtce.org.uk
Council for Scotland	www.gtcs.org.uk
Council for Wales	www.gtcw.org.uk
Council for Northern Ireland	www.gtcni.org.uk
Independent Schools Council	www.isc.co.uk

HELPFUL GUIDES AND RESOURCES

www.direct.gov.uk
This provides an official guide to schools, colleges, and universities

www.ilovethatteachingidea.com
Ideas that teachers have used and want to share with other teachers.

www.into-teaching.co.uk
A useful website for those considering the PGCE route. Includes tips to help you through the course.

www.teach.gov.uk
A list of all the teacher training providers, along with other useful information.

www.teacherexpress.com
Hundreds of useful links are provided here. It lists educational publications, references, resources and other websites.

www.teachingideas.co.uk
Loads of useful primary teaching ideas to use in the classroom.

www.teachingpets.co.uk
Teaching resources for primary school teachers.

www.tes.co.uk
This is the *Times Educational Supplement* website. It is packed full of information on jobs, news, resources and lots more.

QUALIFICATIONS AND CURRICULUM INFORMATION

Council for the Curriculum Examinations and Assessment in Northern Ireland
www.ccea.org.uk

Learning and Teaching in Scotland
www.ltscotland.com

National Curriculum Online
www.nc.uk.net

Qualifications and Curriculum Authority
www.qca.org.uk

Qualifications, Curriculum and Assessment Authority for Wales
www.accac.org.uk

Scottish Qualifications Authority
www.sqa.org.uk

TEACHING ORGANISATIONS

Association of Teachers and Lecturers (ATL)
www.askatl.org.uk

Association of University Teachers (AUT)
www.aut.org.uk

Educational Institute of Scotland (EIS)
www.eis.org.uk

National Association of Schoolmasters Union of Women Teachers (NASUWT)
www.teachersunion.org.uk

National Union of Teachers (NUT)
www.teachers.org.uk

FURTHER READING

How to Complete your UCAS Application, 18th edn (Trotman, 2006)

'One of the most unexpected joys of teaching is when students sometimes graduate into friends. I'm still in regular contact and socialise with a number of my former students and even act as stand-by babysitter for one of them! It's quite scary, though, when they recall what you were like in school ...'

Gill O'Donnell, former teacher

Directory of Teacher Training Courses 2007, 3rd edn (Trotman, 2006)

'An excellent directory.'

Phoenix